Buddhism

For

Beginners

Table of Contents

Introduction: _____ 8

   What this book is not: _____ 15

   What you can expect from this book: _____ 17

   Flower Sermon _____ 18

Chapter 01: What is Buddhism? _____ 20

   The man who brought Buddhism to life: ____ 25

   The Buddha _____ 25

   The early life and transformation of Siddhartha Gautama. _____ 26

   The distinction between ordinary human awareness and Enlightenment _____ 33

   How to prepare yourself for Buddhism _____ 36

Chapter 02: The foundations of Buddhism 39

   Buddhism in the modern-day _____ 42

   How Buddhism is evolving in the modern world: _____ 47

   The fundamental teachings of Buddhism ___ 48

   • The Three Jewels: _____ 50

- The Four Noble Truths: _____ 57
- The Twelve-linked Chain of Causation: _____ 58
- The Three Characteristics Of Existence: ____ 60
- The Noble Eightfold Path: _____ 62
- The Three Fires: _____ 63

What is the goal of the path of Buddhism? ___ 64

Chapter 03: Divisions Of Buddhism _____ 67

The core differences. _____ 71

Chapter 04: Theravada Buddhism _____ 75

Means of realizing Enlightenment _____ 78

Chapter 05: Mahayana Buddhism _____ 82

The Bodhisattva _____ 85

The turning of the Dharma Wheel _____ 88

The Buddha Nature _____ 89

Mahayana Scriptures _____ 91

Distinctions among different sects of Mahayana Buddhism _____ 92

- Tibetan Buddhism: _____ 93
- Zen Buddhism: _____ 93

- Pure Land Buddhism: 94
- Nichiren Buddhism: 94
- Tendai: 95

Chapter 06: Vajrayana Buddhism — 96

God, Goddesses and other Deities in Buddhist Tantra — 99

Chapter 07: Other Forms of Buddhism — 104

Zen Buddhism — 105

What is Zazen? — 107

Overcoming the first hurdle of zazen and Zenspeak. — 109

Tibetan Buddhism — 111

Tibetan Buddhism Scripture — 119

The Bardo Thodol — 120

What makes Tibetan Buddhism so unique? — 122

Pure Land Buddhism — 126

How Pure Land works: — 130

Amitabha — 131

Jodo Buddhism _____ 134

Jodo Shinshu Buddhism _____ 134

Chapter 08: The Key Concepts of Buddhism _____ 136

Karma _____ 137

Nirvana_____ 139

Suffering _____ 140

Reincarnation _____ 143

How does reincarnation work? _____ 146

Chapter 09: The Four Noble Truths _____ 153

The First Noble Truth: Dukkha _____ 154

The Second Noble Truth: Samudaya _____ 155

The Third Noble Truth: Nirodha _____ 158

The Fourth Noble Truth: Magga _____ 159

Dependent Origination in Buddhism _____ 162

The Twelve-linked Chain Of Causation also called Cause and Effect _____ 167

Chapter 10: The Five Precepts Of Buddhism _____ 172

Developing the Mind and Character with Practice of the Precepts _____ 175

Chapter 11: Mindfulness Meditation Practice In Buddhism _____ 178

- Mindfulness of body _____ 179
- Mindfulness of feelings _____ 181
- Mindfulness of mind _____ 184
- Mindfulness of dharma _____ 186

Using mindfulness to get rid of stress and anxiety _____ 187

Benefits of practicing mindfulness_____ 188

Mindfulness in your everyday life _____ 191

Starting regular mindfulness of the Buddha practice_____ 193

Chapter 12: Making Mindfulness Part Of Your Life_____ 197

Creating your meditation and yoga space __ 198

Chapter 13: Benefits Of Buddhism Practices _____ 200

Conclusion_____ 207

Additional Study Resources _____ 211

Introduction:

Buddhism is gaining a lot of popularity in the West, perhaps more than ever before in human history and with good reason. Although it is most predominant in Asia, Buddhism has been widely embraced in the United States of America. It can, in fact, be traced back several generations to the first Chinese and Japanese immigrants in the mid-1800s. Influencers such as D.T Suzuki and the poets of the Beat generation helped to popularize it. However, even though Buddhism has been practiced in the West since the early 19th century, for most people, it's still very confusing and foreign. What makes the understanding of Buddhism tough is the frequent misrepresentation of this religion in magazines, books, social media, and popular culture. Learning about Buddhism can feel extremely difficult if you don't have a lot of solid and ethical foundation to go by. As if that's not bad enough, going to a Buddhist temple or Dharma center may not actually be the best solution. Depending on where you go, you might end up receiving a version of Buddhism that's only applicable to that school. If you're just starting out, this isn't a good thing because first, you need to educate yourself on the full spectrum of the religion before making an informed decision on which aspect resonates most with you.

So let's start here:

Buddhism, unlike any other religion, is hugely diverse. Arguably more so than Christianity. And even though all of Buddhism shares a core of fundamental teaching, it's very possible that much of what you might be taught by one teacher could be directly contradicted by another.

Then there's the other big problem of the scripture. While most of the great religions of the world have one canon of scripture that everyone accepts as authoritative, this doesn't apply in Buddhism. There are three separate scriptural cannons - one for Theravada Buddhism, one for Mahayana Buddhism and one for Tibetan Buddhism. These further divide and sub-divide into various sects within those three traditions often diversifying even further their own ideas about which scriptures are worth studying and which aren't. So having a goal to learn more about Buddhism and converting into this way of life is very good and noble. But you must, as with all things in today's world, educate yourself before making an informed decision on which form of Buddhism you will practice.

As the world continues to be seized by all kinds of crisis and more and more people fall into depression, anxiety, loneliness, trauma, and other stifling conditions, smart individuals are seeking solutions beyond conventional medicine. Many people are choosing to turn to Buddhism and its practices as a guide to the path of peace, enlightenment, and happiness.

Although one can find several articles online and books that talk about Buddhism, most of these resources don't seem to be concise or practical enough when it comes to teaching what people really want to know. Too many questions go unanswered. Many of the things spoken of aren't useful enough for someone living in Brooklyn, Connecticut or Long Beach. Worse still, some of the vernacular used can be very tough to decipher.

If you are among those smart individuals looking to make Buddhism a way of life but you're struggling to find a simple guide to help you get started, you're in luck. This is precisely where you need to be, and this book will help pave the way for your new lifestyle. "Buddhism for Beginners" contains all the answers you need to become a modern-day Buddhist, regardless of your location, vocation, ethnicity, and background. Buddhism for Beginners is a must-read for anyone getting started on this quest of finding peace and happiness because it seeks to take you through the basic and core practices of Buddhism in a way that beginners like you would easily comprehend. By the time you're done reading this book, you will be more in tune with the possibility of infinite happiness that is now available to you. Where other publications fail to teach you how to tune in to that new reality, this book will strive to deliver on that promise. You will learn everything you need to know from the Key concepts of Buddhism to Modern Buddhist practices of Mindfulness, Zen, and Meditation practices.

In Buddhism for Beginners, we travel this unchartered path together and go in-depth into the Buddha teachings, Buddha-nature, and the goal of living a Buddha life. You're also going to learn about core Buddha practices of Karma, Suffering, Nirvana, and Reincarnation. Most importantly, this book will explain the mindfulness and meditation practices of Buddha through which you can project yourself into a life of clarity, peace, and happiness.

I know I'm making big and bold promises here, but if you are interested in leading a qualitative life and attaining utmost happiness, Buddhism can help you realize your desire. Buddhism for beginners promises to serve as a practical guide and offer the answers you need if you have no idea how to begin making this shift.

After years of battling childhood trauma, loneliness, and depression, I decided to become a student of life and seek out alternatives because therapy wasn't getting me anywhere. Subsequently, being a keen student of life for over a decade has made me realize that an awakening is taking place. Although the masses are still bogged down by ordinary experiences, there are those of us who are slowly beginning to awaken.

There was a time in my life where I couldn't sleep without popping pills. My health was getting worse by the day; my familial relationships were in shambles. Each time I tried to start dating, I would end up in yet another abusive relationship. It seemed like the only possible reality for me was that of deep suffering and lots of loneliness. Today I have a beautiful marriage with the love of my life. My health has never been better, and I can't even remember the last time I needed to take any medication for any ailment. Although my childhood experiences and the trauma I was subjected to didn't go anywhere, I have learned to stop recreating that reality. In other words, I entered the path of awakening and watched as my life transformed before my very eyes.

The awakened existence isn't easy; learning to live above ordinary human awareness is almost an art and requires a masterful teacher to show you how. Buddhism is that masterful teacher if you ask me. This book is the channel through which you will now receive your curriculum and insights from your teacher so you can fully awaken into the being you were meant to be.

What this book is not:

If you are not genuinely looking to change yourself from the inside out and walk the journey of personal transformation, then this isn't the right book for you. Buddhism for beginners is here to help you shift in consciousness and take personal responsibility for your life. It's not about shifting blame or letting yourself off the hook for the conditions and quality of life you lead.

This book is also not meant to constrain you into a religious belief system. One of the first myths you must overcome if you want to enjoy the benefits of being a Buddhist is to understand that Buddhism is not a belief system. The doctrines of Buddhism are not meant to be blindly believed. There's a Zen saying, " The hand pointing to the moon is not the moon." I like to think of doctrines more like hypotheses to be tested. They point us to the truth. Buddhism is the process by which the truths of the doctrines may be realized by you.

Although Buddhism is considered a religion with over 500 million followers around the world, it is more than that. Buddhism is not a quick fix; it is a way of life. Westerners often argue whether Buddhism is a religion or philosophy since it isn't focused on worshiping God or gods. We know that in the western world, the norm in every religion is that there should be a God to worship. Well, let me clarify that for you. In a scripture called Kalama Sutta, the Buddha taught us to not blindly accept the authority of scriptures or teachers. He also said we should not judge the truth of things by relying on logical deduction, reason, probability, "common sense," or whether a doctrine fits what we already believe. So if you've come here with that approach, you'll need to shed them off even before we get started.

But what's left if you let go of all that? Glad you asked. The only thing left will be the process or the Path to your Enlightenment.

What you can expect from this book:

As you read through each chapter, you will naturally receive answers and explanations from the teachings of Buddhism that help you understand and make sense of the world around you. Many of the injustices and inequalities happening around the world will not seem as overwhelming anymore. And you will have a practical code of practice or a way of life that leads to true inner peace and happiness. You will discover in this book that Buddhism has answers to many of the problems we are facing in our modern materialistic society. Although Buddhism changes from country to country due to customs and culture, this book is focused on giving you the essence that binds all the different types of Buddhism together. We call it - the Dhamma or truth. Regardless of where Buddhism is practiced in the world, the fundamental truth will always remain the same, and that is what you need to grasp, comprehend, and implement into your affairs. Whether you are looking to solve health, financial, relationship, or career problems or if you are looking to develop your spiritual nature and lead more enlightened existence, this teaching will cater to you.

Flower Sermon

This is a story of the origin of Zen Buddhism, which we'll dive into later in the book. But this famous story is told originally in Chinese whereby Śākyamuni gives a wordless sermon to his disciples by holding up a white flower. No one in the audience understands the Flower Sermon except Mahākāśyapa, who simply smiles. Within Zen, the Flower sermon communicates the ineffable nature of tathātā (suchness), and the smile signifies the direct transmission of wisdom without words. A similar story is then shared in the Eleusinian Mysteries where the story is told of the Buddha who did his own version of the famous Flower Sermon.

One day the Buddha

The ball is now in your court. Daybreak is here, and you no longer need to accept a life of darkness and confusion. As the night sky bows and gives way to daylight, as the sun rises each morning, your life is about to step into the light and clarity that you've always wanted to experience. To get started on your journey and enter a life experience devoid of stress and anxiety with a clear and free mind, let's begin with the fundamentals of Buddhism.

Chapter 01: What is Buddhism?

A simple summing up of what Buddhism is can be described in the following way. It is a practice; a path to spiritual enlightenment and freedom. Buddhism is a path of development that is meant to offer you deep insights and unveil the universal secrets that lead to higher awareness and knowledge of the truth. This is a religion but perhaps not in the sense that we are used to in the western world. What I mean by this is that unlike most other religions, Buddhism is not fixed, rigid, or exclusive to any person. Buddhism is so different in its approach to religion that some people question whether it is a religion at all. For example, the central focus of most religions is one or many, and most are defined by their beliefs. Buddhism is non-theistic because the Buddha taught that believing in gods wasn't very useful for those seeking to realize enlightenment. The Buddha also said that merely believing in doctrines or blindly accepting them just because they are in scripture or taught by priests should not be allowed. Instead, you are to realize the truth for yourself. The focus of Buddhism is on practice, self-discipline, and self-mastery rather than belief. The path by which we arrive at that desired end result of enlightenment is called the eightfold path which we'll discuss in greater detail later in the book.

There's an ongoing experience within the Buddhist teachings that are thousands of years old and still evolving, which has created an incomparable resource for those walking this path. The ultimate desire for all who travel the path of Buddhism is, of course, enlightenment or Buddhahood. When we speak of enlightenment, we are referring to an individual who has awakened and sees with absolute clarity, the nature of things just as they are. That which is real is seen and known for what it is, and that which is transient is also recognized for what it is. Such an individual, also called an enlightened being learns to live life naturally and fully immersed in the present moment according to that clear vision which emanates from within. This is the main goal we all strive to attain when we embark on the journey of becoming Buddhist. Suffering, as we know it in human civilization comes to an end for those who successfully reach this goal.

The basic tenets of Buddhism are pretty straightforward, easy to understand, and very practical. They are: Nothing is permanent or fixed. Each action has a corresponding consequence. Change is possible.
As you can see, Buddhism makes itself accessible and applicable to all people of all ages, race, background, and ethnic culture. And even though these teachings were developed thousands of years ago, we can see they were just as practical and applicable then as they are today. They offer us the change to go within and transform our experience of life so that

ultimately we can become fully responsible for our actions and our lives.

A man stood in front of a microphone in a room full of technologists and scientists waiting his turn to ask Dr. Deepak Chopra a question at the Google conference talk where Dr. Chopra had just completed sharing insights about spirituality. The man sounded a little nervous when he began to speak. It took a while before he summed up the courage to ask the main question, which was: " As an engineer, I tend to be very far removed from religion or spirituality. Based on your teachings, however, I am beginning to wonder if there is a way for me to find the peace I have been seeking and also to figure out a way to deal with the overwhelm that I often experience as I try to make sense of why the world is the way it is. Why are there so many children dying of hunger? How can there be so much devastation in the world, and how can I not get overwhelmed by it, especially since I feel like I can't fix any of it?"

I was moved by how deeply wounded the man felt, and quite frankly I think this is a common theme many westerners can speak to. But what moved me, even more, was the response that Dr. Chopra gave most compassionately. He gave quite a long answer. Too long to recount here. But the most poignant part was this. The key solution to end social suffering and the current depletion of our planet's health is for each one of us to invest heavily on personal transformation.

Personal transformation is the only way to create social transformation and lasting change in the world. This is pretty much what Buddhism is all about. Ending your suffering is the best way to "fix" the wrong in the world, and that is what Buddhism for beginners wants to help you accomplish.

Now, before we can hope to start walking the path that will ultimately lead to Buddhahood, I think it wise to digress a little and speak about the man (yes he was a man, not a god) who brought this philosophy to life.

The man who brought Buddhism to life:

The Buddha

Here's something that startled me the first time I heard it. Buddha isn't actually someone's name, like John or Brenda. It is a tile with a meaning. The word Buddha literally translated means "one who is awake." And yes there is one man who is credited with starting Buddhism, but his name was Siddhartha Gautama. He was born in Nepal around 2500 years ago and actually changed his name to Buddha years later as he received enlightenment.

So who was The Buddha?

When we ask this question, let us come from the right perspective and avoid falling for the myths and false notions associated with Buddhism. The Buddha was not a god or a prophet, and he never made any claims of divinity. He was a man who, like us, got deeply troubled and curious about life. So he sought out answers and became enlightened, understanding life in ways few of us ever do. Before we can fully appreciate the gifts his work has brought into the world, let's look at his early life when he was just as "asleep" as the rest of humanity.

The early life and transformation of Siddhartha Gautama.

Siddhartha Gautama was born in Nepal around 567 B.C.E, into the royal family of a small kingdom on the Indian-Nepalese border just below the Himalayan foothills. His father was a chief of the Shakya clan. It is believed that astrologers and trusted sages prophesied that he would become either a universal monarch or a great sage. Gautama's father, of course, desired his son to become a great king and reign as his successor not some wandering fortune teller. So he did what any loving father would do. He protected his son as much as possible and decreed that Prince Siddhartha should love in luxury and never see the world of pain outside the palace. This was his attempt at ensuring that his son never sees the need to be religious. Sarangis, spice, silk, and every other form of luxury that would satiate the senses of any other man were provided for the young prince. He was entertained by dancing girls, instructed by Brahmins and trained in archery, swordsmanship, running, swimming and wrestling. But as he grew, so did his curiosity. All the luxury in the world could not satiate the curiosity and the unanswered questions that filled prince Siddhartha's mind. Questions such as what is life? Why are we here? Is this all there is? When he came of age, he married Gopa who bore a son, and by all accounts, he should have been the happiest man in the world. Even today, he would be considered very auspicious. Yet he still felt restless, incomplete, as though something was still missing.

By all historical reports, Siddhartha Gautama had a royally privileged upbringing (as one might imagine), and all was fine until the day he desired to go and explore the ground beyond the palace walls. For the first time, he was allowed to go into the city riding a shielded carriage, but that wasn't good enough for him. Instead, he managed to escape the wagon and found himself wandering down the streets of Kapilavastu where what he encountered horrified him. Nothing had prepared him for this experience. He witnessed sickness, old people, and a dead corpse. His charioteer who found him looking lost and distraught told him that all human beings are subject to illness, old age, and death. This deeply anguished the young prince who was still in complete shock.

Here was a young man who had been cushioned from the woes of this world by a well-meaning father who thought protecting his son was the best way to secure a successful life for him. And yet as soon as the young man caught a glimpse of what life was really like outside his bubble, he knew the inevitable would quickly fall on him too. No amount of luxury and comfort could keep away things like old age and death.

As they made their way back to the palace, the prince noticed a wandering ascetic walking peacefully along the road, wearing the robe and carrying the single bowl of a sadhu. This was the first sign of peace he had witnessed all day and so figured it must be the best path to take for him to get the answer to the problem of suffering. Despite the inner restlessness, Gautama had felt before leaving the castle walls, we can assume life was good. But when he realized how different life was outside the boundaries of his luxurious palace as well as the harsh facts of the inevitable things in life such as death and suffering, something stirred within him. The bubble created around him burst. He contemplated deeply, trying to understand the meaning of life and when he couldn't come to terms with the shallow answers that surrounded him, he felt compelled to leave the palace life and his wife and child to follow the traditional Indian path of the wandering holy man with one intention - seeking the truth.

- In search of freedom:
In his quest for freedom, Gautama investigated a variety of teachers and practices including atheists, materialists, idealists, and dialecticians. He then settled on working with two teachers, one of whom was named Arada Kalama. This teacher had three hundred disciples and taught Gautama how to discipline his mind and enter into the realm of nothingness, which was very useful for him but certainly not the end. So he moved on to work with Udraka Ramaputra who taught him how to concentrate his mind to a level where he was

neither conscious nor unconscious. While this was indeed a marvelous skill, it still didn't offer the answers or freedom Gautama was in search of, so he kept moving on. For six years, Gautama and his five companions continued to practice austerities and concentration. From what I've read, this journey of truth-seeking and learning from various teachers made Gautama very proficient at practicing austerities and concentrations. He showed himself no mercy - living with just a single grain of rice a day. You see in ascetic teachings, their core belief was that one could free the spirit and find truth by denying the flesh. Gautama took on this belief and practiced it with such extremity that he almost starved himself to death. With a near-death experience and having forsaken all fleshly pleasures, including food, one might think he had finally solved his puzzle. But the truth is, the mysteries of life and death were still just as elusive as before. Real understanding seemed out of reach, and so he abandoned this practice and decided to look elsewhere for answers. He made the decision to stop punishing his body and started eating again (at which point his companions abandoned him), and he gave up asceticism altogether.

After regaining his strength and nourishing his body, he decided it was time to seek for answers the one place he hadn't: in his own heart and mind. Going by the commonly shared story of how the last phase of his personal transformation occurred, Gautama went and sat under a fig tree (the Bodhi tree) with his legs crossed. Unmoved like the mountain, after having listened to and learned from various teachers all that information did not seem to lead him to the answer he wanted. So he decided to trust in his intuition and learn from direct experience rather than looking externally for answers. According to the traditional story, Gautama vowed to stay there until he'd gained Enlightenment. After many days (some records say seven days, others say seven weeks), he received Enlightenment. It is said that he woke up at the age of thirty-five and became the Buddha, the Awakened One, known as Shakyamuni, the sage of the Shakyas. We are told that for several weeks, he simply enjoyed his new state of enlightenment and freedom without sharing his knowledge because he felt it was too complicated and difficult for people to understand. But legend has it that Brahma, chief of the three thousand worlds requested that the Awakened One teach those whose eyes were only a little clouded over, the Buddha agreed and the rest, as they say, is history.

The distinction between ordinary human awareness and Enlightenment

If ordinary human experience consists of childhood experiences, psychology, opinions, and perceptions, then Enlightenment is unconditioned. In Buddhism, it is believed that

Siddhartha Gautama reached this unconditioned state of being that goes beyond anything else in the world. That is what transformed him into the Buddha.

A Buddha is free from judgment, greed, hatred, resentment, and ignorance. The defining character qualities include peace, wisdom, compassion, loving-kindness, and freedom. The reason Enlightenment is such a big deal to those of us seeking truth is that it brings insight into the deepest workings of life. In so doing, the problems that we face, the things that torture and cause us to suffer for so long all lose power. This is what Gautama experienced. The issue that had initially set him on his spiritual quest was finally resolved. For the remaining forty-five years of his life, he lived on as the Buddha that we know, traveling through most of northern India, spreading his understanding and sharing his message.

In the East, his teaching is known as the Buddha-dharma, which can be translated into 'teaching of the Enlightened One.' The Buddha preached and taught people from all walks of life. He had his own disciples, many of whom gained Enlightenment as well, and nowhere is there any mention of exclusivity in his teachings. Because of how open and welcoming his teaching is, his disciples have continued to pass it down and evolve it from generation to generation, right down to the present day. So in case you ever wonder whether the Buddha was some extraterrestrial or someone with capabilities that are out of your reach, I hope this story has helped you see that he was just like you and I. A man longing to end suffering and to understand life. He was willing to struggle and find truth against all odds, and through that perseverance, he was able to discover a simple path accessible to all of us. Now it's time to discover his teachings and apply it to your life story. But before you can call yourself a Buddhist, there are a few things you must clearly understand.

How to prepare yourself for Buddhism

The higher your understanding, the easier it will be to transform yourself. This practice is more than merely reading a few books, calling yourself a Buddhist, and making superficial changes in the way you live your life. It's about wholly integrating the teachings with your mind. To do this, you must first prime your mind, cultivate spiritual stability, and reconnect all aspects of your being. This is referred to as renunciation. In Tibetan Buddhism, renunciation (Nges-Jung) implies that you must first come to the realization that you are caught in the process of rebirth in samsara. In Buddhism, samsara is often defined as the endless cycle of birth, death, and rebirth. More commonly understood as the world of suffering and dissatisfaction or the opposite of Nirvana. Therefore as you begin your practice, you must recognize and realize the true nature of samsara itself and how you exist in it. You must become acutely aware of the unsatisfactory nature of samsara and the conditions that surround your life. This is the first and essential step on your journey of studying and mastering the Path.

The fully renounced mind is the prerequisite to practicing Buddhism effectively. The moment you become sufficiently disillusioned by your samsara, from the depths of your heart, you will have that undeniable aspiration to free yourself from it. This will be a pure, spontaneous, and constant aspiration that is referred to as renunciation in Buddhism. There are two ways of developing a fully renounced mind. The first is to meditate on the two aspects of samsara - the nature of suffering and the cause of this suffering. The second way is to meditate on the twelve links of interdependent origination, which you will learn about as the book unfolds.

Bottom line, this study of Buddhism and your commitment to walking the path cannot be something haphazard if you want to experience personal transformation genuinely. The mind and heart must be all in, and this is something you commit to with all your being. This is what will lead to the insights, breakthroughs, and solutions that the teachings can deliver to you. Read the coming chapters from that mindset, and you will "get it." Fail to prepare your mind in this way, and this will turn out to be yet another form of entertainment that might make sense but certainly won't transform you from samsara to freedom.

Chapter 02: The foundations of Buddhism

The Buddha taught that we live in a fog of illusions and that you and I and the world around us are not what we think we are. He explained that confusion is what leads us to create problems and in so doing, we fall into unhappiness, suffering, and sometimes destructiveness. The only way out of the confusion, the only way to gain freedom from the illusions that surround us, is to intimately and individually perceive for ourselves that they are mere illusions.

Believing in a doctrine won't cut it. Trying to use logic to understand the teachings we are about to get into won't help you find the answers you seek. This is why many of the doctrines and practices don't make much sense at first. They are not logic-based and do not conform to our habitual thought patterns. But just think about this for a moment. If these practices and teachings conformed to how you already think, how would they help you break free from the box of confusion?

The doctrines are meant to challenge your current understanding of life and who you are. That's why we are told of various times when the Buddha refused to answer direct questions, such as "do I have a self?" or "how did everything begin?" The reason he sometimes refused to answer these questions is that he felt the question was irrelevant to realizing enlightenment. He wanted people to stop getting so stuck in views and opinions. So right now, I want you to do the same. Suspend judgment, prejudices, opinions, and trying to make logical sense of everything before diving deep into the teachings of the Buddha. I think this will be an essential step to enabling yourself to be in the receptive mode as we expand on the foundations of Buddhism, the teachings of the Buddha and the different forms of Buddhism being practiced today. Although forms vary in the modern-day, know that the essence of Buddhism or what is known as the Dharma always remains constant no matter where you practice it.

After the Buddha passed away around 438 B.C., his followers started organizing religious movements, and the Buddha's teachings became the foundation for what would develop into Buddhism, as we know it. In the 3rd century B.C., the Mauryan Indian emperor who was known as Ashoka the Great decided to make Buddhism the state religion of India paving the way for missionary work and Buddhist monasteries. This lead to further awareness and expansion of the faith, which spread far beyond India. The thoughts and philosophies of Buddhists started to differ as followers began integrating ideas differently. The core essence of the teachings has still been preserved, but I'm sure you can agree with me that 2,500 years is a relatively long time. So as times changes, cultures evolved and religion continued to spread, so too did Buddhism evolve with its followers.

Buddhism in the modern-day

Buddhism continues to spread rapidly around the world. There are many Buddhist centers across various European countries, not just in the western capitalist countries but also in countries like Poland that are more socialists. Buddhism is also growing in South Africa, Australasia, North America, and South America. To me, the most significant appeal for Buddhism, and one of the reasons that led me to convert is because it is spiritual, practical, and scientifically based as well. The Buddha said, "Do not believe in anything I say just out of respect for me, but test it for yourself, analyze it as if you were buying gold." I think for many of us living in this modern society, we want the ability to think, choose, and decide for ourselves what is truth and what isn't. We want to be free of the dogma often associated with religion.

Buddhist leaders such as His Holiness the Dalai Lama, continue to host open dialogues with scientists to investigate what reality is. Buddha said that all problems come from not understanding reality; from being confused and ignorant about life. If we were aware of who we are and how the world we exist in operates, we would not create problems out of our confusion. Hardly any other religion in the world possesses such an open attitude in examining what is true. For example, His Holiness the Dalai Lama has said that if scientists can prove that something Buddha or his followers taught is incorrect or just superstition; he would be willing to drop it from Buddhism. This type of open-mindedness is obviously very attractive to modern individuals, especially in the Western world.

The other attractive feature in Buddhism is the fact that it is dynamic and can be adapted to suit the needs of any society. In the past, learned masters have adapted Buddhism to the culture of each society where it spread. This is why, as you'll see in an upcoming chapter, we have more than a singular form of Buddhism. In today's world, where modern countries differ from each other and from ancient civilizations, Buddhism is being presented in slightly different ways. As a general rule, Buddhism emphasizes a rational explanation. Within this context, however, various points and approaches require more emphasis depending on predominant cultural traits. Even the Buddha recognized the fact that variety was necessary because no two people think in exactly the same way. So he offered a variety of methods as he traveled across India. Think of it this way, if there were only one type of food available in a country, it would not appeal to everyone. If on the other hand, different foods could be had with varied flavors, everyone could find something desirable to eat. This was the intention behind the diverse methods that Buddha taught. He wanted to cater to a broader spectrum of people with varying tastes and still give each one the chance to develop and grow based on his or her nee

In countries like Switzerland and the United States of America, for example, where psychology is a big thing, teachers of Buddhism usually present it from the point of view of psychology. In countries like Latin America and most of Southern Europe where people prefer a devotional approach, Buddhism is introduced in a devotional manner because in general people there enjoy chanting. In Northern Europe, however, people don't chant, so teachers of Buddhism tend to emphasize a more intellectual approach. If you consider the current state of Eastern Europe where the general tone is somber, melancholic and perhaps even sad, Buddhist teachings are much appreciated because there it is presented in a way that helps uplift their spirit. It teaches them methods for working on themselves, which heals their wounds and fills up the emptiness that is often felt. So in this way, Buddhism adapts itself to the culture and mentality of the people in each society while simultaneously preserving the core teachings of Buddha. The principal instructions are never changed, and the main objective is always kept. What is the primary goal you ask?

To overcome all of our limitations and problems. And to realize our fullest potential as individuals so that we can develop ourselves to the point at which we can also help everyone as much as possible. Since the aim is to overcome limitations and realize our potential, whether practitioners do this with more emphasis on the intellectual, psychological, scientific or devotional approach becomes less significant as that depends mainly on the culture.

How Buddhism is evolving in the modern world:

As modern-day individuals, we have changed a lot, especially when it comes to traditionally accepted consumer behavior. If you look at the business world, things are shifting drastically because most business owners don't know how to adapt to the new behaviors of the consumer. Today's consumer will not buy something without a little research and examination. Google and social media are where many turn to before making a decision on where they should travel, what car they should get etc. So even when it comes to religion, most people want to make sure it's a religion or philosophy that makes sense before converting. Blind faith does not cut it anymore. And I think Buddhism is so appealing to many of us because it's one of the few religions that's open to this type of scrutiny and examination. Like science, Buddhism asks us to verify all that we hear and learn for ourselves. We must, through personal experience, prove or disprove it; only then should we make a decision about it. That was how I started. I released the need to make assumptions, wore my curiosity hat, and took it one step at a time. Testing to see if, through my experimentation, I could experience the results many teachers speak of.

That is what I now invite you to do. As we start to break down the teachings, don't just take them at face value, ignorance is not bliss, and blind faith is not part of what we promote in Buddhism. So do your due diligence and self-experiment to find your truth.

The fundamental teachings of Buddhism

The Buddha did not teach that God created the Universe. Instead, he pointed to a great Law or what is known as Dharma. In Buddhism, Dharma means cosmic law or order. But the

Dharma is so much more than a label for Buddhist doctrines. It comes from the ancient religions of India and is found in Hindu, Jain teachings and Buddhism. Although there can be no accurate translation of the word into English, its original meaning is something like "natural law." The root word 'Dham' from which it is derived means to "uphold" or "to support".

Broadly speaking, we can say Dharma is that which upholds the natural order of the universe. Walpola Rahula, a Theravadin monk, and scholar, wrote, "There is no term in Buddhist terminology wider than dhamma. It includes not only the conditioned things and states but also the non-conditioned, the Absolute Nirvana. There is nothing in the universe or outside, good or bad, conditioned or non-conditioned, relative or absolute, which is not included in this term." [What the Buddha Taught (Grove Press, 1974), p.58]

By living in accordance with this Law, true Wisdom, compassion, and hence, freedom from suffering may be achieved. Suffering is inevitable in life and can only be overcome by confronting it and living through it. Depending on where you do your research, you might find some modern-day teachers presenting the Buddha's teachings as separate while other consider all his core teachings and summons (which were numerous), as one thing. For the sake of simplicity, I intend to treat the teachings of Buddha as one unified whole and break each down to easily digestible concepts. Namely:

• The Three Jewels:

Becoming a Buddhist involves taking refuge in the Three Jewels according to Buddhist tradition. Also known as the Three Treasures, the Triple Gem or the Three Refuges, these are the ideals at the heart of Buddhism. There's even a formal ceremony of Ti Samana Gamana also known as "taking the three refuges" which is performed in nearly all schools of Buddhism. But you don't need a formal ceremony if you feel ready to follow the Buddha's path. There's a simple beginner's statement that you can already recite to embark on this journey today. But before sharing that statement of oath, let's talk about the Three Treasures. They are the Buddha (the yellow jewel), the Dharma (the blue jewel), and the Sangha (the red jewel). By making these three central principles in your life, you become a Buddhist.

The Buddha or yellow jewel refers to both the historical Buddha and the universal ideal of Buddhahood itself. It also involves making a commitment to yourself in the pursuit of Enlightenment or Buddhahood which means that you aim to become someone who sees the nature of reality absolutely clearly, just as it is and that you will live fully and naturally in accordance with that vision. This is the goal of the Buddhist spiritual life. It was the goal of the Buddha, which he ultimately achieved, and that is why the whole Buddhist tradition regards him as the root founder, guide, and inspiration for all to emulate. By achieving Buddhahood, all suffering ends.

The Dharma, as I mentioned earlier, primarily means the entire teachings of the Buddha or the truth he understood (amongst other various meanings). But the most critical meaning I want you to grasp is that Dharma (as a term for you), should mean the unmediated Truth as experienced by the enlightened mind. Your Dharma shall be made known to you as you walk this path. Dharma is also used in Buddhism to refer to the teaching that was born when the Buddha first taught his sermon after receiving enlightenment. This occasion is traditionally referred to as 'the first turning of the wheel of the Dharma', and the eight-spoked Dharma wheel is a common emblem of Buddhism in this regard.

Another common way you'll find Dharma being used in Buddhism is to refer to the scripture canon, which includes records of the Buddha's life, scriptures from a later date and the written teachings of those people who have attained Enlightenment over the centuries. The whole canon is vast and just as long and significant as the Christian Bible and represents the literature of unparalleled riches. One last meaning of Dharma I want to make you aware of before moving on is that it can also be used to mean the practices that are outlined within the scriptures. As the Dhammapada says, this can be summed up as, "learning to do good; ceasing to do evil; purifying the heart." Emphasis is placed on teaching Dharma across all schools to help us develop mindfulness and kindness. In practicing Dharma, we learn to examine our actions in light of our ethical values and see how our thoughts condition our lives.

The Sangha is the third jewel that's all about spiritual community. Broadly speaking it also refers to the people with whom we share our spiritual lives. If we are to commit to achieving Enlightenment and practice the Dharma, we need guidance and support, especially from others who have done so before us. We also need the friendship of other practitioners, and in Buddhism, this becomes even more necessary because Buddhism isn't an abstract creed or philosophy. It is a way of approaching life, which means people play a significant role in this. Sangha includes all the Buddhists in the world and all those of the past of the future. They are all there to support and guide you on this path, so you are never alone.

Aside from this, Sangha in Buddhism also incorporates archetypal figures known as Bodhisattvas. For example, Manjusri is the embodiment of Wisdom, and he is depicted carrying a sword with which he cuts through ignorance. Avalokitesvara is the embodiment of compassion, and he's depicted with four, eight, or a thousand arms with which he seeks to help all living beings. All enlightened teachers, as well as the Bodhisattvas, are collectively known as the Arya Sangha (community of the Noble Ones).

Before moving on to another core element of Buddhism, I want to bring back your attention to this concept of taking refuge in the Three Jewels. Here are three lines you must recite to begin the Buddhist life.

I take refuge in the Buddha.
I take refuge in the Dharma.
I take refuge in the Sangha.

What does it mean to take refuge?

Depending on which school of Buddhism you receive your teachings, the meaning of taking refuge may vary slightly. Zen teacher Robert Aitken wrote in his book "Taking the Path of Zen," that taking refuge in the Three Jewels is more of a vow than a prayer. He tells us that the original Pali words of the three "I take refuge" lines that I just shared above can be literally translated as I will undertake to find my home in the Buddha, the Dharma, and Sangha. And by finding my home in the Buddha, Dharma, and Sangha, I can free myself from blind conditioning and realize true nature.

Bhikkhu Bodhi, a Theravada teacher, said, "The Buddha's teaching can be thought of as a kind of building with its own distinct foundation, stories, stairs, and roof. Like any other building, the teaching also has a door, and in order to enter it, we have to enter through this door. The door of entrance to the teaching of the Buddha is the "going for refuge to the Triple Gem." That is, to the Buddha as the fully enlightened teacher, to the Dhamma as the truth taught by him and to the Sangha as the community of his noble disciples."

This isn't about evoking some supernatural spirits to come and save you. It's a personal vow and commitment that you make for yourself. In the words of yet another teacher, Tibetan Buddhist, and professor of Indo-Tibetan Buddhist studies at Columbia University - Robert Thurman - " Remember that awakening, freedom from suffering, salvation if you will, liberation, omniscience, Buddhahood, all come from your own understanding, your insight into your own reality. It cannot come just from the blessing of another, from some magical empowerment, from some sort of secret, gimmick or from membership in a group."

I think that's a great reminder beginners need to hear over and over again because sometimes we get seduced by the allure of gurus and magical incantations.

• The Four Noble Truths:

The central doctrine of Buddhism is said to be these four noble truths which provide a conceptual framework for all Buddhist thought. These are the truths understood by the 'worthy ones,' those who've attained enlightenment. The Four Truths are dukkha (the Noble Truth of Suffering), the arising of dukkha (the Noble Truth of the Origin of Suffering), the stopping of dukkha (the Noble Truth of the Cessation of Suffering), and the path leading to the ceasing of dukkha (the Noble Truth of the Way Leading to the Cessation of Suffering). These four noble truths are considered the fundamental teachings of the Buddha, and I have dedicated an entire chapter to orientate you into the teachings of these four noble truths.

• The Twelve-linked Chain of Causation:

Simply stated and closely connected to the understanding of the four noble truths is the basic teaching. It is the law of cause and effect. They are Ignorance, volitional formations, consciousness, craving, grasping, becoming, rebirth, name, and form, the six sense organs, feeling, contact, aging, and death. The Buddha recounted that on the night of his enlightenment, he awoke to the profound nature of the twelve links of dependent origination. Clearly seeing how beings trap themselves in an endless cycle of self-perpetuating confusion and misery. He went on to claim that nobody could understand his teaching without understanding the nature of these twelve links. That's a challenge in and of itself even for Dharma practitioners who've been at this for a long time because these twelve links remain a very elusive subject, something difficult to fully penetrate. It's even more challenging to try and relate them to one's own personal experience and daily practice. For a while, I was relegating this topic to the "too hard" pile. But after much study, debate, and contemplation, I do have some beginner insights to share that might aid you on your journey as well. In the chapter where I cover the Four Noble Truths, I share my insights as well as those of the masters that are helping me bring more light into this dense subject.

• The Three Characteristics Of Existence:

The first is change or impermanence. Originally taught as anicca. The Buddha taught that "all compounded things are impermanent."
This teaches us that nothing in this world is fixed or permanent. We are not the same people either physically, emotionally, or mentally that we were a year ago (even an hour ago). We are dynamic ever-evolving and changing beings living in an ever-changing world. As such, it is pointless to struggle or fight for lasting security.

The second is suffering. We know from the previous chapter that Dukkha, otherwise translated as suffering (though in a different form), is the very reason the Buddha set off on his great spiritual quest. Dukkha doesn't necessarily mean suffering the way westerners define the term. Dukkha implies the generally unsatisfactory and imperfect nature of life, which is a broad spectrum that also included the issues we are faced with today. Since we are always experiencing change, attachment to anything is futile and can only lead to suffering. However, you should know that Buddhism doesn't teach that life is all suffering. Buddhists do believe that there is happiness in life. But they know just like everything else, it is not permanent. Even in the most prosperous life (think of the Buddha's childhood, for example), there is suffering. Happiness is subject to the same law of change and impermanence.

The third characteristic is that there is no such thing as the self. There is no - 'I'. This is a bit tricky to explain, but I try my best. In Buddhism, we do not believe that there is anything unchangeable or everlasting in the human being. In other words, there is no stable sense of 'I' to anchor yourself in. The whole concept of 'I' is basically a false concept of the self trying to establish some stability in an unstable and temporary collection of elements. You see what we are taught in Buddhism is that we are all made up of various elements that form to make a human being. 'I' am made up of various skandhas (aggregates), i.e., rupa-skandha (form), vedana-skandha (feeling-sensation either pleasant, unpleasant or neutral), sankhara-skandha (volitional mental activities), sanna-skandha (perception), vinnana-skandha (sense consciousness).

These are the three seals of Buddhism and form part of the Noble Eightfold path.

• The Noble Eightfold Path:

This wheel of the Dharma with eight spokes represents the Noble Eightfold Path. They are - Right View, Right Thought, Right Speech, Right Action, Right Livelihood, Right Effort, Right

Mindfulness, and Right Concentration. More on this later.

• The Three Fires:

The Buddha gave a famous Fire Sermon where he said, "Your house is on fire, burns with the Three Fires; there is no dwelling in it." The house refers to the human body. The three fires that burn are Desire, Anger, and Delusion. These powerful energies that we can all relate to are called 'fires' because untamed (which is the case for most of us), they can bring a lot of harm and hurt to ourselves and others around us. That is not to say there are bad and evil as most extremists think. The teachings of the Buddha state that when properly calmed through spiritual training, these three fires can be transformed into the genuine warmth of real humanity.

What is the goal of the path of Buddhism?

Zen teacher Sheng-yen gave a direct answer to this question that really resonates with me. He said, "Buddhism has no goal. It's just that people of this world need it, so it gives people something. It doesn't need to have a certain goal. You see of all the people of this world, some know there are afflictions, and others do not know. So all Buddhism does is point out humans' fundamental problem. Even if people are ignorant of them, afflictions still exist. If you know there are afflictions, you still don't know where they come from. So, pointing out this problem, showing the root of the affliction and how to resolve them, that is the goal of Buddhism."

Of course, if you ask others within the Buddhist community, you'll get very different answers. Some consider nirvana to be the ultimate goal of Buddhism. Other's think the goal is to understand dukkha and end it permanently. For others, the goal is to see things just as they really are with absolute clarity. None of these goals are wrong.

That's why I revert back to the response given by the venerated Master Sheng-yen. Given our understanding that Buddhism is a practice; a way of life that deals with personal transformation, self-purification, and realization of one's truth, I would argue that the ultimate goal of Buddhism could also be something very personal encompassed by the overarching noble truths taught by the Buddha.

Buddhism places a considerable amount of emphasis on self-reliance and personal transformation. The main goal for all Buddhist practices is to bring about the same awakening that the Buddha achieved through an ongoing transformation of the heart and the letting go of the concept of 'I'. So then, the question that is most relevant to you understanding Buddhism shouldn't be "what is the ultimate goal of

Buddhism" as that would imply that Buddhism has its own secret agenda. Instead, start asking, "what is my ultimate goal in walking this Buddhist path?" And as long as you keep aligned with the fundamental teachings of the Buddha, you are sure to experience your highest and best potential and finding Enlightenment.

Chapter 03: Divisions Of Buddhism

Over the years, Buddhism has evolved into different forms. One thing we must always bear in mind is the fact that Buddhism isn't monolithic. As such, when it spread through Asia thousands of years ago, it divided into several sects each with its own rituals and canon of scriptures. This is why we will find doctrinal disagreements as we move from one school of thought to another.

While most blogs on the web today will try to convince you that there are many schools of Buddhism and to some extent they are right, the fundamental truth is there are only two (though some argue three) primary schools of Buddhism. And within these main schools can be found more subdivisions but at a core level, each school practices the essence of the historical Buddha teachings. I will focus on teaching you about the two leading schools of Buddhism and give as many examples as possible of the different types and subdivisions that can be found all over the world. I am also sharing another resource at the end of the book to help you figure out which school of Buddhism is right for you.

The three primary schools of Buddhism are Theravada, Mahayana, and Vajrayana. But in essence, there are only two because as you will see, Vajrayana is actually founded on the philosophy of Mahayana Buddhism.

What creates this separation between these schools of Buddhism?
To understand that, we must trace the Buddhism steps back into the past. Although much about early Buddhist history isn't very clear it seems that sectarian divisions began to crop up shortly after the death of Siddhartha Gautama, the Buddha. Buddhist councils were summoned to debate and settle doctrinal

disputes so that everyone could stay on the same page but to no avail. About a century or so after the death of the Buddha, two significant schisms emerged. In fact, this split is sometimes called the Great Schism. The two that emerged were called Mahasangaika (of the great sangha) and Sthavira (the elders). You might also find some referring to Sthavira as Sthaviriaya or Sthaviravadin (doctrine of the elders). Okay, so that was a really long time ago (2nd or 3rd BCE), but in today's world, Theravada Buddhism is considered direct descendants of the latter school. When it comes to Mahayana Buddhism, which hadn't yet emerged, many would argue that Mahasangika would be a forerunner for this school of thought, but recent discoveries speak of a more complex picture. Today's Mahayana carries a bit of Mahasanghika DNA, but it also bears traces of long-ago Sthavira sects. It appears that Mahayana has roots in several early schools of Buddhism, and somehow, these roots converged.

The reason for the split remains unknown. According to Buddhist legend, the split occurred when a monk named Mahadeva proposed five doctrines about the qualities of an arhat to which the assembly at second (or third depending on who you ask) Buddhist Council could not agree. This is, of course, speculation. Another plausible cause that could have led to the break up is the Vinaya-Pitaka or rules of the monastic orders. Sthavira monks supposedly added new rules to the Vinaya, and the Mahasangika monks did not consent. I am sure there were various other issues, but I think we have enough knowledge of the past to step back into the present and increase our understanding of these two schools of Buddhism in modern-day. Besides, how and why the split took place isn't relevant to us. On this path of seeking truth and liberating ourselves from the suffering that has led us to this moment, our main concern is transformation. Gaining a little history knowledge of where your studies originate is encouraged but certainly shouldn't concern you too much.

The core differences.

The core doctrinal difference that separates Theravada from Mahayana comes down to how they interpret anatta. Anatman or anatta is the core Buddhist doctrine that teaches there is no self. At least not in the sense that we have been accustomed to. This is the doctrine that makes Buddhism so different from other spiritual traditions such as Hinduism, which maintains that Atman, the self, does exist. The full comprehension of this doctrine is of paramount importance to you as a student of Buddhism as it is the key that will unlock the meaning behind most of the teachings of the Buddha. But don't get me wrong, just because I stress the importance of understanding it doesn't mean it's easy to do it. The teaching itself is simple but not easy to comprehend, especially for those of us living in the western world. Anatta is often misrepresented, misunderstood, and easily overlooked because of the layers of complexities that are involved in the unpacking of this concept. So before moving on with the rest of this chapter, let us attempt to unpack (at least somewhat) what this core doctrine is about, notwithstanding that you probably won't get much of it until you're further into your studies.

The teachings of the Buddha speak of Anatta, as "there is no self" which many assume implies that nothing exists, but that's not accurate. There is existence but not in the way we think. In other words, what you think you know and what you think you are is actually a delusion that's getting in the way of you understanding reality. With anatta, although there is no such thing as self or soul, there is still afterlife, rebirth, and manifestation of Karma, which is why right actions and right thought are vital if you wish to gain freedom. So what we know from the teachings of Buddha is that there are three characteristics of existence, which I highlighted previously. Anatta (absence of self) is one of these three as we saw. The other two are anicca and dukkha. As long as we continue to live from an awareness of having a sense of self, which usually stems from living purely through the five Skandhas, we shall continue to cling to things and consequently prolong our suffering.

Shifting gears once more to figure out what divides the two primary schools of Buddhism we find that in Theravada tradition, it is taught that true understanding of anatta is only attainable by the practicing monks. Ordinary people cannot possibly understand it because of the psychological difficulty. One must apply the doctrine in all areas of life, deny their own self completely and that of others. Theravada teaches that nirvana is a state of anatta. And even within the Theravada community, there are those who dispute this and claim that nirvana isn't just a state; it is the true self.

On the other hand, the Mahayana tradition takes the concept of anatta even further. They teach that anatta must be achieved by all and that the end result is to accept emptiness. Nagarjuna saw that the concept of a unique identity leads to selfishness, possessiveness, and pride. If you want to be free from these common obsessions, the only way is to eliminate the self entirely. Failure to do so will keep you stuck in ignorance and the cycle of rebirth. Another significant difference you'll notice is that with Theravada tradition their key thing is arhat - the individual who has realized enlightenment whereas in Mahayana their key thing is the enlightened being who is dedicated to bringing all beings to enlightenment. Now that you have an understanding of the core differences in these two doctrines let's discuss each a little more.

Chapter 04: Theravada Buddhism

Theravada Buddhism means the "Way of the Elders" and is considered to be the oldest form of Buddhism being practiced today. It is sometimes referred to as the Southern School of Buddhism because it's most dominant in countries like Sri Lanka, Cambodia, Thailand, Myanmar, and Laos. Theravada draws its teachings from the earliest Buddhist teachings in history recorded in the Pali Canon. It developed from a sect called Vibhajjavada what was established in Sri Lanka in the 3rd century BCE.

As with the other schools of Buddhism, Theravada believes in this notion of the cycle of birth or rebirth from one life to the next that we call Samsara. The ideal goal here for you should be to realize that all is thought and escape from the Dukkha and ultimately attain

Enlightenment and Nirvana. But here, Theravada takes a different turn because it is much closer to some of the original practices that we see with Siddhartha Gautama, the Buddha.

Self-Power and Individual Enlightenment

What I mean is that with Theravada, it is a very personal journey. It is about the individual and taking personal responsibility. Enlightenment takes place through meditation, perhaps with a little help from some teacher. Therefore enlightenment can only come through one's own efforts without help from gods or other outside forces. It's also about recognizing the non-self and realizing that we are all one. Ultimately, either in this life or a future life, one achieves Nirvana. The aim of Theravada is to become an arhat. An arhat is a person who has realized enlightenment and freed himself from the cycle of birth and death.

There is also a diverse interpretation of anatman. Theravada considers anatman to mean that an individual's ego or personality is an illusion. Once one is freed of this delusion, he or she may enjoy the bliss of Nirvana.

It is important to know that in Asia, there is a bigger difference between monastic and ordinary people who practice Theravada. Monks meditate, study and teach; ordinary people in general (with a few exceptions) practice by supporting the monasteries with alms, chants, prayers, and donations. They are also encouraged to keep the five precepts (will mention them below) and observe uposatha days. In the Western world, those who come to Theravada as adults most commonly practice Vipassana or "insight" meditation and study the Pali Canon. The Pali Canon is the main body of scripture for Theravada and the only accepted one for this school of Buddhism. As a result, we can start to see the differences even in how certain words will be pronounced. For example, in Theravada Buddhism, you will see the word dhamma instead of dharma, or sutta instead of sutra. This is because Theravada uses Pali instead of the Sanskrit form of standard terms. You can find more about the Pali Tipitaka on the resource section as well.

When it comes to divisions within this school of Buddhism, the difference is minimal because as I said, Theravada has a strict adherence to the original teachings and rules of monastic discipline. But there are variations in practice from one temple to another.

Means of realizing Enlightenment

The primary means of achieving enlightenment in the Theravada tradition is through meditation. There are two forms of meditation in Theravada. Samatha or "calming" meditation and Vipassana or "insight" meditation.
Samatha is the earliest form of meditation and isn't actually unique to Buddhism. It is used to

make the mind calmer and temporarily take the person to higher jhanic states. Vipassana emphasizes disciplined self-observation your body and thoughts and how they interconnect. It is used to achieve insight into the nature of things, which at first can be very difficult because of our preconceived notions, options, and past experiences. The purpose of practicing Vipassana is to change the way we perceive and understand the universe altogether. Unlike the temporary changes experienced by Samatha, any changes experienced through Vipassana will be lasting. A follower of Theravada Buddhism is expected to abstain from all kinds of evil, accumulate only that which is good and purify his or her mind. Although there are many rules contained within the Vinaya, there are five precepts that are undertaken by those adhering to a Buddhist way of life. Namely:

• Refrain from harming living beings.

• Refrain from taking that, which is not freely given.

• Refrain from sexual misconduct.

- Refrain from wrong speech, including lying, idle chatter, malicious gossip, or harsh speech.
- Refrain from intoxicating drink and drugs, which lead to carelessness.

Of course, the code of conduct for laypeople is less strict than that for monks. Laypeople are mostly expected to follow the precepts mentioned above and support the monasteries. Monks and lay followers have a very strong relationship. It is part of the tradition and a way of mutual support. The people supply food, medicine, and cloth for robes and monks give spiritual support, blessings, and teachings. However, this is not a mechanical transaction. It is more a natural openhearted giving. For example, monks are not allowed to request anything from laypeople, and laypeople cannot demand anything from the monks. It's a system that has been functioning well in most Theravadan countries, so monks are usually well taken of relative of course to the wealth or poverty of the local people.

Chapter 05: Mahayana Buddhism

Mahayana Buddhism means the "Great Vehicle." My research and studies have led me to the conclusion that the Mahayana teachings arose to help people deal with some of the problems they were having to deal with while on the Buddhist path. Some very wise and sensitive individuals who followed the path set forth by the Buddha founded it. They wanted to make Buddhism available for everyone and to teach differently so that individuals of any temperament could have a chance to engage the dharma. It is said that that the Mahayana sutras came from the Buddha and his immediate followers, even though they are very different in tone and style from the original Pali Canon. As far as experts can tell, they are most certainly later writings, but that's okay. Buddhism is an evolving system of teachings and awakenings that don't necessarily have to come directly from the Buddha to be valid.

Around the 1st century BCE, the name Mahayana began to be used to draw a distinction with Hinayana or the lesser vehicle. This shows an emerging emphasis on the Enlightenment of all beings in contrast to individual Enlightenment. But even then, Mahayana as we know it did not yet exist as a separate school. It wasn't until much later that we experienced a full formation of this school of Buddhism.

This form of Buddhism is dominant in countries like China, Taiwan, Tibet, Japan, Nepal, Mongolia, Korea, and most of Vietnam. It's actually not a single group but a collection of traditions such as Zen Buddhism, Pure Land, and Tibetan Buddhism. Mahayana Buddhism encompasses an extensive set of various practices and can be quite complicated, but the generally accepted idea here is that you will have help as you try to attain Enlightenment. I see it as a more flexible tradition that regards many new scriptures composed in the early centuries CE as authentic. It is tough to make any blanket statements about Mahayana that would hold true for all of Mahayana teachings. For example, we know that most Mahayana schools offer a devotional path for lay followers, but it doesn't mean they don't have monastic schools as well. Some schools are centered on a meditation practice, while others expand meditation with prayer and chanting.

Therefore while in Theravada (as we have just seen) the ideal is to achieve Enlightenment as an individual through pure meditation and prioritize nothing else until that happens, in Mahayana, the ideal is slightly different. It's not even necessarily about you attaining Enlightenment or entering the state of Nirvana, but it's about getting as close to it as you possibly can and then assisting others to do the same. So the real goal for those practicing Mahayana tradition is to become a Bodhisattva.

This term is used in both schools of Buddhism. In Theravada is means someone who is still trying to become an Arhat whereas, in Mahayana, it means someone who has almost achieved Nirvana but now puts it on hold to help other sentient beings achieve Nirvana. While Theravada and Mahayana are both rooted in the basic teachings of the historical Buddha and both emphasize the individual search for freedom from the cycle of samsara, the methods are very different. In Mahayana, the path is about becoming a Bodhisattva.

The Bodhisattva

In Mahayana, the Bodhisattva is the ideal way for a Buddhist to live. The Bodhisattva is motivated entirely by Karuna (compassion) and informed by Prajna (deep wisdom). We are told that anyone can embark on the bodhisattva path, which is a way of selflessness and a sincere wish for all beings to be freed from suffering. This ideal for the Mahayana tradition (to enable all beings to be enlightened together) is more than just compassion even though we know that is fundamental to Buddhism. It's more because we understand our interconnectedness and therefore realize how impossible it is to separate ourselves from one another.

According to Mahayana teachings, you need six perfections to become a Bodhisattva.

- The perfection of giving and generosity.
- The perfection of ethical conduct or behavior.
- The perfection of patience.
- The perfection of vigor and diligence.
- The perfection of meditation.
- The perfection of wisdom.

Mahayana Buddhism is also more "religious" than classical Buddhism in general (which is usually purely philosophical) because it ascribes to the worshiping of specific deities. We'll get into that in a little while.

This school of Buddhism was the first significant tradition to enter the United States of America. The Chinese and Japanese immigrants who arrived in the nineteenth century primarily introduced it. In the present day, there are two main subdivisions stemming from Mahayana tradition that you've no doubt encountered. These are Zen Buddhism and Pure Land Buddhism, both of which have Asian-American and Euro-American practitioners. Here's an excerpt of the Bodhisattva vow that depicts the primary intention.

However, innumerable sentient beings are, I vow to save them. However inexhaustible the defilements are, I vow to extinguish them. However immeasurable the dharmas are, I vow to master them. However, incomparable enlightenment is, I vow to attain it.

The turning of the Dharma Wheel

Mahayana also teaches the Three Turnings of the Dharma Wheel but is more focused on the Second Turning. Theravada Buddhism is philosophy based on the Buddha's first turning in which the core practice is egolessness or emptiness of self.

The first turning was the teaching of the Four Noble Truths and other elements of Tripitaka, which was the beginning of Buddhism. The second turning was the doctrine of sunyata or emptiness. This is a cornerstone of Mahayana teachings whereby all dharmas are seen as emptiness (sunyata) and without inherent reality. It's not just the ego, but all reality is considered an illusion. Emptiness and compassion form bodhicitta, which is an epitome of Second turning. The Third Turning was the Tathagatagarbha doctrine of Buddha Nature, which is another cornerstone of Mahayana that emerged around the 3rd century CE. There is also a philosophy called Yogacara that was originally developed in a Sthavira school named Sarvastivada. This also forms an essential milestone in Mahayana history. Sunyata, Buddha Nature and Yogacara are the chief doctrines that set Mahayana apart from Theravada.

The Buddha Nature

Teaching not found in Theravada but upheld in Mahayana is the teaching that Buddha Nature is the immutable nature of all beings. That all sentient beings are inherently connected to the Buddha, the ultimate source of everything. But this Buddha Nature is covered by the attachments and sufferings of life, so in order to be set free, one must "uncover" this hidden truth

There are various interpretations of these teachings from one Mahayana school to the next, and depending on where you study, you might learn to see Buddha-nature as a seed or potential. Or you might learn to see it as fully manifested but unrecognized because of your illusions. This teaching usually comes in the study of the third turning of the Dharma Wheel and forms the basis of the Vajrayana, which we'll discuss in the next chapter. It is also taught in the esoteric and mystical practices of Dzogchen and Mahamudra.

Mahayana tradition also says that there are three aspects of Buddhahood, which it describes by regarding Buddha as having three bodies (trikaya).

Dharmakaya body, also known as Dharma body, which can be translated, as "Buddha is transcendent." He is the same thing as the ultimate truth or the absolute nature of all beings. Sambhogakaya body, which can be translated as "Buddha's body of bliss or enjoyment body. In this enjoyment body, Bodhisattva appears in a celestial realm. Nirmanakaya body, also known as the material body of Sakyamuni Buddha, which can be translated as "Buddha's earthly body." He had an earthly body just like any other human being or in other words, he manifested in human form. This doctrine is what molds the belief in a Buddha nature that is inherently present in all beings and which can be realized through the right practices.

Mahayana Scriptures

The Mahayana teachings are based on Tibetan and Chinese Canons. As I said earlier, Theravada follows a single scripture called the Pali Canon, which is said to include only the actual teachings of the Buddha. But the Chinese and Tibetan Mahayana canons have added a vast number of sutras and commentaries that are strictly Mahayana in addition to some of the shared Pali Canon texts. Of course, Theravada disregards these sutras as they do not consider them legitimate. Some of the sutras include the Prajnaparamita and Lotus sutras. Mahayana also uses the Sanskrit form of standard terms instead of Pali like Theravada Buddhism.

Distinctions among different sects of Mahayana Buddhism

There are several types of Buddhism practices that seem to be entirely different religions, yet they are all built on the same Mahayana doctrinal foundation. The doctrinal differences among these schools are minor compared to the differences in practice. Most people who choose to join a particular Mahayana school do so because a particular style of practice resonates with them. In Western culture, especially, Mahayana is the foundation supporting most of the various types you may have encountered. Here are a few of the most common ones but keep in mind this list is far from complete.

• Tibetan Buddhism:

This type of Buddhism has amassed a massive following in recent years, especially in Western culture. There are four major schools and many more sub-schools of Tibetan Buddhism. Tibetan Buddhism combines meditation with ritual, chanting, and other practices. One of its most distinctive features is the fact that it utilizes tantra or deity yoga. What this means is that with Tibetan Buddhism, identity with tantric deities is employed as a means to Enlightenment.

• Zen Buddhism:

This is the Japanese name of Chan, a sect that originated in China during the 6th century. Chan Buddhism also spread to Korea and Vietnam. Zen Buddhism has been mostly a monastic school for much of history, although there is also a long tradition of laypeople practicing it too. The most basic practice of Zen is a mindful, silent meditation practice called Zazen.

• Pure Land Buddhism:

This is also known as Amitabha or Amida Buddhism and emphasizes faithful devotion to the Buddha Amitabha. The most distinctive practice of Pure Land referred to as Nianfo in Chinese and Nembutsu in Japanese is the mindful recitation of Amitabha's name. It is taught that by the grace of Amitabha, one may be reborn in the Pure Land where Enlightenment can be realized. The place from which it is easier to enter Nirvana.

• Nichiren Buddhism:

This is also a Japanese tradition that has been gaining a large following in Western culture. It is focused on mindful chanting practices that evoke the mystical power of the Lotus Sutra to bring all beings to enlightenment.

• Tendai:

This type of Buddhism is the least known and practiced in the western culture, but it is a long-established Mahayana tradition well known in Asia. It offers a number of meditation and other practices to enable enlightenment.

In chapter seven of this book, I dive deeper into Tibetan, Zen, and Pure Land Buddhism. But for now, I want to give a little attention to the tantric focused school of Buddhism - Vajrayana - which is also founded on the Mahayana tradition.

Chapter 06: Vajrayana Buddhism

Vajrayana Buddhism is a term that describes the tantric or esoteric practices of Buddhism. This form of Buddhism is founded on Mahayana philosophy and can be more accurately understood as an extension of Mahayana. It is known the "Diamond vehicle" and also referred to as Esoteric or Tantric Buddhism. It is often associated with Tibetan Buddhism as well as a Japanese school of Shingon. The term Vajrayana seems to have appeared around the 8th century. When it comes to diversity in Buddhism, this form is truly unique because of its approach to rapid Enlightenment through the use of tantras.

What Are Tantras?

The term tantra can mean a variety of things depending on the particular Asian spiritual tradition you are referring to. Broadly speaking, it refers to the use of ritual or sacramental action to channel divine energies. Within Buddhism, tantra is usually a means to enlightenment through identity with tantric deities. The deities are archetypes or enlightenment and also of the practitioner's own fundamental nature. Through meditation, visualization, rituals, and other means, the practitioner realizes and experiences himself or herself as a deity. To successfully make this happen, the student must master a series of increasingly esoteric levels of teachings and practice over a period of years. This requires the guidance of a master teacher or a guru. Please don't attempt a DIY approach with this at that wouldn't be a wise choice.

The Vajrayana Buddhist practices are very intense, so I do not recommend it as a starting point for beginners. In fact, most Vajrayana schools only accept advanced teachers and students. It is important to note that Vajrayana strives to maintain secrecy within its teachings to protect both the students and the teachings. The esoteric nature of tantra is considered necessary because teachings at each level can only be understood by someone who has mastered the previous level. If you were to stumble upon a tantra without full preparation, not only would you not "get it," chances are you'd misrepresent it to other - something Vajrayana attempts to avoid at all cost.

Much of Vajrayana is built upon a kind of synthesis of Madhyamika and Yogacara schools of Mahayana philosophy. The school focuses most on the Sunyata doctrine and the Two Truths doctrine. It is said that at the highest tantric levels, all dualities are dissolved including the illusion of appearance and emptiness.

God, Goddesses and other Deities in Buddhist Tantra

When we go into a temple, we often see many statues of deities and various Buddhas and Bodhisattvas. We often hear the names of a great many Buddha and bodhisattvas. Why are there so many of them in Buddhism? And what about God? Are there gods in Buddhism? There is no simple yes or no answer to this question. The answer is both yes and no depending on who you ask and the context surrounding that question.

Buddhism does not believe in a God or gods in the usual sense of the word as it is frequently used in Christianity and other religions. This is a non-theistic or "atheistic" religion, which means that believing in a God or gods is not really the point. It doesn't believe that a particular god created the world and humans. Instead, we are taught that this world as we know it has emerged as a result of the collective karma created by sentient beings in countless worlds for eons.

Karma is ever-changing, and so are people, so we and the world were not created by a god but by our own karma. This is known as karmic origination. It is considered a type of atheism, but in appearance, it seems to be a polytheistic religion. Mainly because there are all kinds of god-like creatures and beings called devas populating the early scriptures of Buddhism and schools like Vajrayana Buddhism still makes use of tantric deities in its esoteric practices. There are also Buddhists who believe that devotion to Amitabha Buddha will bring them to rebirth in the Pure Land. Indeed there is a contradiction here when it comes to giving a clear answer on this topic, but hopefully, by the time you're done with this chapter, you'll have received a little more insight on how to understand the numerous statues of Buddhas, bodhisattvas, and deities.

Southern Buddhist countries like Sri Lanka and Burma have only one Buddha statue others have multiple that come in all shapes and sizes. Their Buddha statue is that of Shakyamuni Buddha. They also have Dharma-protecting deities, for example, the four-faced Buddha.

In Tibet, they have even more Dharma-protecting deities that are all manifestations of the bodhisattvas and Buddhas. The variety of forms makes it seem as though there are countless statues, but a Tibetan's belief focuses on the transformation body of his own deity. In Chinese Mahayana Buddhism especially, there are all kinds of deities. In the major sutras such as Ksitigarbha Bodhisattva, Avatamsaka, and lotus sutras, when Shakyamuni is teaching the Dharma, we see deities, arhats, bodhisattvas, and pratyeka-buddhas as well as the Dharma-protecting deities commonly referred to as the eight divisions of divinities. Actually, as depicted in the name Buddhism, we only worship and acknowledge the Buddha nothing else. Buddhahood is achieved by sentient beings, and a bodhisattva is one who is in the process of going from the phase of sentient beings to Buddhahood. Bodhisattvas work with Buddhas and help Buddhas to deliver sentient beings. The deities protect the Three Jewels, which we talked about in chapter two. By safeguarding the Three Jewels and Buddhism, it continues to exist and flourish in the human realm. The Buddhadharma can be smoothly navigated, and many beings can be safely delivered with the help of the deities to ensure this is done without any hindrance. They are also meant to help bring peace to those following Buddhism. In the Lotus Sutra, the Bodhisattva sutra and the Avatamsaka Sutra it is said that these bodhisattvas and deities will offer protection to those studying, reciting and practicing Buddhism. For that reason, we will find in monasteries many statues of deities, bodhisattvas, and Buddhas.

Shakyamuni Buddha introduced many Buddhas. There is a sutra of the names of three thousand Buddhas, and we are also told that there were seven Buddhas in the past as well as the five ancient Buddhas of the five directions. Some teachers also speak of the three Buddhas of the period - the Buddha of the past, present, and future. The Three Bodies of the Buddha (dharma body, reward/bliss body, and transformation body) and those of the three directions - the Medicine Buddha of the East, Amitabha of the west and Shakyamuni of the Saha World. These three come together to form the great Buddhas, all of which was identified by Shakyamuni Buddha in the sutras. In Mahayana, especially Chinese Mahayana Shakyamuni is regarded as the principle and central Buddha and therefore, the founder of Buddhism. That's primarily due to the fact that he introduced the various bodhisattvas, Buddhas and deities that we see in monasteries today.

Chapter 07: Other Forms of Buddhism

As we said earlier, Mahayana is complex and has further divisions and sects within its teachings with varying practices. Although I won't go into all the different factions, I feel confident that after this you'll have greater clarity on the distinctions within the various schools and the practices they follow. Please note that even with all this explanation, you probably won't find each and every temple you visit fitting perfectly into my description. You might also come across temples that seem to combine practices of more than one tradition. Many sects come in a multitude of denominations, so always keep an open, flexible mind whenever you visit a temple or get introduced to a particular school. As long as you have a deep understanding of the core teachings, you'll be just fine.

Zen Buddhism

I'm sure you've heard of Zen Buddhism before. You may have even had a moment of Zen (occurrences of insights and a feeling of connectedness and understanding that seem to come out of nowhere). But what is Zen?

By scholarly definition, Zen is a school of Mahayana Buddhism that emerged in China about 15 centuries ago. In China, Zen is called Ch'an Buddhism. Ch'an is the Chinese translation of the Sanskrit word dhyana, which refers to a mind absorbed in meditation. "Zen" then, is the Japanese rendering of Ch'an, and even though many languages have their own terms, the ultimate translation of the word Zen is always -Meditation Buddhism. Some scholars suggest that Zen was originally the end result of the marriage between Taoism and traditional Mahayana Buddhism. The sophisticated meditative practices of Mahayana met the no-nonsense simplicity of Chinese Taoism had an offspring - a new branch of Buddhism that is today known everywhere. And while I am going the general route of classifying all of Zen as one school of thought just for the sake of simplicity, be aware that in practice it is way more elaborate with many traditions. So if you do go down the route of becoming a Zen Buddhist, you'll need further knowledge and teachings on the specifics of the various Zen traditions.

The Zen definition of itself.

So I gave you a scholarly definition of Zen. Let me now give you an understanding of how Zen defines itself. The Indian sage Bodhidharma, who is called the First Patriarch of Zen, defines Zen in the following way. " A special transmission outside the scriptures; No dependence on words and letters; Direct pointing to the mind of man; Seeing into one's nature and attaining Buddhahood."

Zen is sometimes said to be the face-to-face transmission of the dharma outside the sutras. Throughout history, teachers have transmitted their realization of dharma to students by working with them face-to-face, making the lineage of teachers vital. In fact, a genuine Zen teacher can easily trace his lineage of teachers back to Bodhidharma and at times all the way back to the historical Buddha and beyond.

Bodhidharma also taught that Zen isn't something intellectual that can be learned from books or any other intellectual discipline. It is a practice of studying the mind and seeing into one's nature. The primary tool used in Zen Buddhism is known as Zazen.

What is Zazen?

This is a form of meditation. Zazen is a Japanese word, and through the daily practice of this meditation, you can develop the foundation of Zen practice. Many YouTube videos and websites offer basics of practicing Zazen, but if you are serious about studying Zen Buddhism, I encourage you to find a community or school where you can regularly practice it with others.

Given the popularity of Zen Buddhism in recent years, many new Zen centers and monasteries have been established. Try to find one near you and if there aren't any available, consider searching for a "sitting group" - where laypeople get together at someone's home and sit zazen.

As with most aspects of Buddhism, it may take a while before you begin to appreciate zazen or even fully get it. At first, you might see it as mind training, and yes it is that and so much more. But it does take a while before you can experience the more that it has to offer. If you stay consistent with your practice, your understanding will soon change and deepen. Expect this to be an intimate and very individual journey. No two people will experience zazen the same way.

Overcoming the first hurdle of zazen and Zenspeak.

In the practice of Zazen, you are required to sit zazen with no goals and no expectations, including the expectation of getting enlightened. For most of us, that's an enormous challenge. A friend of mine told me that when he first began practicing Zen, this was one of his most difficult challenges to overcome. He sat with goals and expectations for months before getting exhausted and finally learned to let go and "just sit."

Then, of course, there was the matter of the language and literature being used in Zen. Much of it won't make sense at first. There is no secret decoder that can help you decipher the literature, it just comes with time. After practicing for a while with your teacher, you'll find it becomes a bit easier to catch on. But I wouldn't recommend accepting many of the explanations you see on the Internet because as

I said before, Zen cannot be an intellectual discipline. It is transmitted from teacher to student; it must be lived. The only way to understand Zen is to face the dragon in the cave. The bottom line when it comes to Zen Buddhism is this: It's not the more significant or more popular type of Buddhism but is highly regarded. It's a very difficult path, especially for laypeople and should not be approached lightly by any means because this type of Buddhism is certainly not for everyone. What I do know is that there's something very alluring about Zen Buddhism. Think about Kung Fu and martial arts, poetry, music, flower arranging, and the tea ceremony. These have all been greatly influenced by Zen. Speaking of which the Indian Sage Bodhidharma is said to have taught at the Shaolin Monastery of China. Yes, you read it right. The famous Kung Fu place we've all heard about in Western Culture. Turns out it was a real place and that indeed Zen Buddhism and Kung Fu have a significant connection. If you like a good challenge and feel compelled to face the dragon, Zen Buddhism might be the right practice for you.

Tibetan Buddhism

Buddhism was a foreign import introduced into Tibet in the 600s from India and China. Over the centuries, it became the dominant cultural form exerting a powerful influence in religion, politics, art, and other aspects of society. But the history of Tibetan Buddhism really began with the Bon religion of Tibet that was animistic and shamanistic in nature. We can still see elements of it to some degree in Tibetan Buddhism. The religious practices found in the ancient Tibetan cultural world included incantation of mystic magical formulas, the exorcism, and destruction of demons, divination, auguries, oracles, and symbols of sacrifice and ransom (many being aspects of Shamanism). When Buddhism took hold of the Tibetan culture, many of these native traditions were incorporated into Buddhism. It is this element within Tibetan Buddhism (magic and supernatural rituals) that's so remote from the original teachings and practices of Buddhism that cause many to refer to it as Lamaism, treating it almost like a separate religion or at the very least, an offshoot of the original Buddhism.

The legendary story of how Buddhism took effect in Tibet is worth recounting, whether it merits full truth or not. It is said that in 641 CE, King Songtsen Gampo unified Tibet through military conquest and took for himself, two Buddhist wives. Princess Bhrikuti of Nepal and Princess Wen Cheng of China are credited with introducing their husband to Buddhism. Songsten Gampo invested in the first Buddhist temples in Tibet, and he also got translators to work on Sanskrit scriptures. In addition to moving people away from the Bon tradition, the King was having trouble building a monastery due to spiritual obstacles. Many years later,

King Trisong Detsen who had become the reigning king invited the famous yogi Padmasambhava to Tibet to subdue the ongoing obstacles (local demons) that were still making it hard to build the first monastery successfully. But instead, he decided to convert them to serve his work in propagating the teachings. In so doing, he set a precedent within the tantric Tibetan Buddhist tradition that even those factors in our life that are seemingly negative can be used as fuel to further our spiritual growth. They do not need to be subjugated or destroyed but incorporated into our path. This is why Padmasambhava often referred to as the precious master is credited with building the first monastery in Tibet and establishing one of the four major schools. The monk Shantarakshita was also invited at around the same time to come and assist with the introduction and teaching of Buddhism into the culture, helping to make it the official religion. According to Barbara O'Brien of Learn Religions, in 836 CE, King Tri Ralpachen, a supporter of Buddhism died, and when his half brother took reigns, Buddhism became suppressed, and the Bon religion was re-established as the official religion once more. That is until a Buddhist monk assassinated the King plunging Tibet into chaos and division. Suffice it to say, they went through some challenging times, and you can read all about the Tibetan Buddhism history in the resource "How Buddhism Came To Tibet."

In today's world, Tibetan Buddhism is associated with the Dalai Lama, who has lived in exile in India since in1959 after the Chinese invasion. There was a time when Tibet was home to the largest monasteries in the world, but as time went by, things changed drastically. Although there's an ongoing debate on whether Tibetan Buddhism is identical to Vajrayana, experts confirm they are not. Vajrayana is taught in Tibetan Buddhism together with other vehicles. Tibetan Buddhism combines the essential teachings of Mahayana (the foundation of Vajrayana Buddhism) with Tantric and Shamanic as well as their ancient Bon religion.

The division within the Tibetan community also amplified the emergence of different groups within Tibetan Buddhism. These four sects all trace themselves back to Shakyamuni in an unbroken chain of enlightened masters and disciples that extend down to the present day. All four sects share an emphasis on the three turnings of the wheel of dharma.

Their difference is more in the lineage the follow and not necessarily a difference in doctrine or practice. Namely:

- Nyingmapa. This was founded by Padmasambhava and is the oldest sect. It is well recognized in the Western culture for the teachings of the Tibetan Book of the Dead. The disciples of Padmasambhava formed Nyingma, which means "ancient" and refers to the fact that they were essentially the first real school of

Buddhism that wasn't Indian in nature but Tibetan. Today this tradition still continues as a heavily yogi-like tradition, existing as the somewhat loose structure of teachers and students.

• Sakyapa was founded by Gonchok Gyelpo (1034-1102CE) when he built a monastery in an area with lots of gray earth (gray earth in Tibetan is Sakya).
His son Gunga Nyingpo became his spiritual successor, which set a precedent for hereditary transmission going forward and is certainly unique in a religious tradition that normally emphasizes finding someone's reincarnation and empowering them as successor.

• Kagyupa was founded by the Indian yogi Tilopa (988-1069 CE). He was an ardent practitioner and became enlightened, developing a system of meditation known as "Mahamudra" or "the great seal." He passed on his teachings on the nature of the mind to the proud academic Naropa who then received a student from Tibet called Marpa. After studying with Naropa, Marpa too the teachings he received back home with him and soon became known as the Great Translator for the great effort it took to make these teachings accessible in his homeland. One of Tibet's greatest yogi saints - Milarepa - was Marpa's chief disciple who then trained Gampopa, who trained the first Karmapa who brought these teachings under the monastic umbrella. Centuries later, Kagyupa tradition is headed by the Karmapa Lama.

• Gelugpa is also known as the Virtuous school and was founded by Tsong Khapa Lobsang Drakpa, also called Je Rinpoche (1357-1419). This is perhaps the easiest tradition for us to recognize, as it is the one headed by His Holiness the Dalai Lama. Before there were reincarnated Dalai Lamas though, there was Atisha, an Indian master who arrived in Tibet at 60 years old. He reinvigorated the monastic community in Tibet and became the founder of the Kadam School. In fact, many of the lineage figures mentioned before all studied in this school. In the 14th century, a monk named Tsongkhapa established Ganden Monastery, at which point the tradition had resurgence and became known as the Gelugpa School. One of Tsongkhapa's disciples became the first Dalai Lama, and these reincarnated teachers have continued to oversee and carry out the traditions of this lineage.

In addition to these older traditions, there's a new lineage that was formed in the United Kingdom known as "New Kadampa Tradition." The Tibetan-born Geshe Kelsang Gyatso founded it. But you should know this particular group is regarded by some Buddhist and non-Buddhist to be outside the mainstream tradition.

Tibetan Buddhism Scripture

From the 11th to the 14th centuries, a lot of effort was devoted to translating every available Buddhist text into Tibetan, and in fact, in the present day, we find that many Buddhist works in their Original Sanskrit did not survive. What survived are the Tibetan translations. The Tibetan Canon is a list of sacred texts recognized by various sects of Tibetan Buddhism consisting of more than 300 volumes and thousands more of individual texts. The Tibetan canon includes earlier foundational Buddhist texts from the Sarvastivada and Mahayana tradition as well as Tantric texts. Bu-ston (1290-1364) did the final compilation of the Tibetan canon in the 14th century and divided it into two parts. The Bka'-'gyur or Kanjyur, which means Translated word, consists of canonical texts. It is made up of 98 volumes with around 600 texts. The first printing of the Kanjur actually took place in Beijing China and was completed in 1411. It wasn't until 1731 that the first Tibetan edition of Kanjur was printed at sNar-tang. The Bstan-'gyur or Tenjur, which means Transmitted word consists of semi-canonical commentaries and treatises by Buddha masters. It contains 3626 texts in 224 volumes and is divided as follows: Sutras - 1 volume; 64 texts. Commentaries on the Sutras - 137 volumes; 567 texts. Commentaries on the Tantras - 86 volumes; 3055 texts.

The Bardo Thodol

The famous Tibetan Buddhist text is the Bardo Thodol, which translates to liberation through hearing in the intermediate state. But you probably know it as the Tibetan Book of the Dead. It's a funerary text that describes the experience of the soul during the interval between death and rebirth (Bardo). Lamas recite it over a dying or recently deceased person or sometimes over an effigy of the deceased.

The Bado Thodol differentiates the intermediate states between lives into three Bardos, which are further subdivided. The Chikhai Bardo or "Bardo of the moment of death" features the experience of the clear light of reality or at the very least a close approximation to it depending on one's spiritual capacity. The second is the Chonyid Bardo or the experiencing of reality, which features the experience of visions of various Buddha forms. The sidpa Bardo or rebirth that features karmically impelled hallucinations, which eventually result in rebirth. The Bardo Thodol also mentions three other Bardos: Life or ordinary waking consciousness, dhyana or meditation, and dream. These six Bardos together form a classification of states of consciousness into six broad types, and any state of consciousness forms a sort of "intermediate state" (intermediate between other states of consciousness. Confused yet? Don't worry, it happens to all of us. As I said at the beginning of the book, understanding comes as you walk the path and if you prepared your mind well enough then sooner or later that which makes no sense at first will suddenly awaken in you and you will know the truth with absolute clarity.

What makes Tibetan Buddhism so unique?

In Tibetan Buddhism practices, there are many rituals and spiritual practices that are unique to this tradition alone. For example, their use of mantras and yogic techniques.

Similar to Mahayana schools, they too have prominent Buddhas and a pantheon of bodhisattvas, and Dharma protectors. Arya-bodhisattvas are able to escape the cycle of death and rebirth but compassionately choose to remain in this world to assist others in reaching nirvana or Buddhahood. Dharma protectors are mythical figures that have been incorporated into Tibetan Buddhism from various sources such as Hinduism and their native Bon religion. Their job is to protect and uphold the Dharma. In this school, however, bodhisattvas are portrayed as both benevolent godlike features and wrathful deities.

They have also developed a strong artistic tradition, paintings, and other graphics that are used as aids to understanding. Visual aids such as pictures, structures of various sorts, and public prayer wheels and flags are prevalent in Tibetan Buddhism and provide an ever-present reminder of the spiritual domain in the physical world. When it comes to relationships and communities, Tibetan Buddhism strongly supports both monastic and laypeople communities. Laypeople are expected to perform various ritual practices at temples, take pilgrimages, and participate in their numerous festivals, funerals, and other important ceremonies. As a non-initiate in Tibetan Buddhism, you may gain merit by performing rituals such as food and flower offerings, water offerings, religious pilgrimages, or chanting prayers. You can also light butter lamps at the local temple or fund monks to do so on your behalf. Tantric practitioners also make use of rituals and objects. Meditation is an essential aspect of Tibetan Buddhism and can be aided by the use of specific hand gestures called mudras and chanted mantras such as the famous mantra of Avalokiteshvara - "om mani padme hum". There are various meditation techniques employed by different sects within Tibetan Buddhism, including dzogchen, mahamudra, and the six yogas of Naropa.

A lama (lama means teacher in Tibetan Buddhism) may make use of a variety of ritual objects, each being endowed with rich symbolism and ritual function. Another important ritual is the Cham. This is a sacred dance of sacred music, healing chants, richly ornamented multi-colored costumes, all of which are masked. Mudras are used by monks to revitalize spiritual energies, which generate wisdom, compassion, and the healing powers of Enlightened Beings. This ritual also has an accompanying narration and monastic debate demonstration, which usually provides a fascinating glimpse of ancient and current Tibetan culture. But you should know that this ritual is forbidden in Tibet due to China's occupation. Qualified practitioners of Tibetan Buddhism may also study or construct unique cosmic diagrams known as mandalas (these have become quite common in the western culture), which assist in inner spiritual development.

As you can tell, there is a strong emphasis on outward religious activities in contrast to other Buddhist schools where the focus is more on the inner spiritual life. Tibetan Buddhism is unique in that it has become one of the most prominent Buddhist strands practiced in the West. Very often, when we speak of Buddhism, we're most likely referring to Tibetan Buddhism. Even yoga studios in America widely propagate elements of the Tibetan Buddhist practice such as mindfulness meditation, which has gained a lot of attention in mainstream media. At the core of Tibetan Buddhism, we find the principal teachings practiced by all other schools. And yet one cannot deny how the country's history, society, and its indigenous religious, cultural practices altered the expression of Buddhism in Tibet. Laypeople practicing Tibetan Buddhism must be diligent in their study to ensure they learn about and practice all the necessary physical rituals. They must also learn to provide material support to the monasteries and rely on the monks to organize their various ceremonies.

Pure Land Buddhism

Pure Land Buddhism, also known as Amidism and Shin Buddhism, is a unique type of Buddhism that has become very popular in the

West. Pure Land is also the most widely practiced traditions of Buddhism in East Asia. It first appeared in China around 150 CE courtesy of the monks An Shih Kao and Lokaksema. With the founding of a monastery on Mount Lushan by Hui-yuan in 402 CE Pure Land gained prominence and rapidly spread throughout China after which it spread to Japan. As it grew, Honen Shonin established Pure Land Buddhism as an independent sect in Japan known as Jodo Shu. Today, it stands as the dominant form of Buddhism in the country. It is founded on the Mahayana Buddhist tradition.

The main aim of Pure Land isn't Nirvana like most other schools but rather a rebirth into an interim "Pure Land" where Nirvana can then be easily accessed. Westerners who encountered Pure Land earlier on started comparing Pure Land Buddhism with Christianity in that the ideal of going to a "Pure Land" sounded similar to the Christian delivery into heaven. In reality, the two are very different. There are three primary texts in this tradition known as "Three Pure Land Sutras," namely: Infinite Life Sutra, Amitabha Sutra, and the Amitayurdhyana Sutra. The Sutras of Pure Land Buddhism center on the figure of Amitabha (Amida in Japanese), one of the five wisdom Buddhas and his Pure Land called Sukhavati. The core teaching of Pure Land Buddhism is that nirvana is no longer practical to attain in today's world. Instead, you should focus on devotion to Amida, which will gain you enough karmic merit to go to the Pure Land of which nirvana will then be just a short step away. It is said that Siddhartha Gautama, the Buddha (or Shakyamuni Buddha depending on your particular school), whose teachings founded Buddhism predicted that people in the future would have too many afflictions and worries which would make attaining Buddhahood in one's lifetime extremely difficult. He felt it would take many lifetimes to achieve such a state and knew help from another Buddha would be essential. In the

Great Collection Sutra, it is taught that the Buddha said that one could succeed in cultivation by learning the Pure Land method. Amitabha Buddha was therefore introduced, as the much-needed helper people were to rely on. Amitabha is there to ensure you don't have to rely solely on yourself to attain enlightenment, as is the case with other vehicles.

There's a certain level of simplicity when it comes to the religious practice of Pure Land that might be the reason it has gained so much popularity. It mostly consists of chanting or repeating a mantra of devotion to Amida " Namu Amida Butsu" as often as possible to reinforce a proper and sincere state of mind and gain admission to the Pure Land at death. Venerable Master Chin Kung said Pure Land method is hard to believe but easy to practice and I think he's right about that. He also said, "The Pure Land method is a shortcut to the ultimate Enlightenment. Using other methods, we take a long circuitous route to achieve

Enlightenment. Seeing birth into the Pure Land is the short cut that ensures us of attaining Enlightenment in one lifetime. From this, we know that this method is outstanding and beyond comparison. All Buddhas, bodhisattvas and past patriarchs have praised this method. It is a rare opportunity for us to encounter it in this lifetime."

According to Master Sheng Yen, all you need is the tripod of faith, vows, and practice, and you'll get your rebirth in the Pure Land. So let's talk a little more about how you can practically and sincerely start practicing Pure Land.

How Pure Land works:

The Pure Land method is mindfully chanting the Buddha-name Amitabha while visualizing Amitabha in your mind. Another technique is visualizing Amitabha's Pure Land as per the Amitayurdhyana Sutra (the land of utmost bliss) or a combination of both. I have included a resource video that walks you through the visualization as depicted on the Amitayurdhyana Sutra to get you going in the right direction (please see resource section - Amitayurdhyana Sutra).

On the surface, Pure Land Buddhism seems to have moved away from the fundamental Buddhist ideas. For example, Amitabha Buddha is sometimes treated as if he were God. Although this may appear so, perhaps the chanting of his name isn't so much a prayer to summon an external diety but more a way of calling out one's own Buddha-nature. However, given that some of Shinran's writing speaks of Amitabha Buddha in a language that many of us would regard as describing God, this is a topic open to much debate.

Amitabha

Amitabha (or Amida in Japanese or Amito-fo in Chinese) means Immeasurable Light is the central figure on Pure Land Buddhism and people are expected to call on Amitabha for help if they want to be reborn in Sukhavati (the Pure Land). The nature of Amitabha Buddha is, of course not very clear, but the mystical view regards him as an eternal Buddha. It is believed that he manifested himself in human form as the historical Siddharta Gautama - The Buddha. The story is that once there was a king who was deeply moved by the suffering of beings in the world that he gave up his throne and became a monk named Dharmakara. Dharmakara was heavily influenced by the 81st Buddha and vowed to become a Buddha himself, intending to create a Buddha-land that would be free of all limitations. After lengthy meditations and study, he set down 48 vows, of which the most important is the 18th vow. This vow states " If I were to become a Buddha, and people, hearing my name, have faith and joy and recite it for even ten times, but are not born into my Pure Land, may I not gain enlightenment."

It turns out he did build a Pure Land and attain Enlightenment. So those that follow his teachings, therefore, recite his name trusting that he will be there to deliver them into the Pure Land.

Fully understanding Pure Land at first glance is a bit tricky. We can look at it as a poetic metaphor for a higher state of consciousness. And that would be very valid as chanting would there be a meditative practice that enables a follower to alter his or her state of mind. Where argument arises is in the face of the importance given to chanting the name in faith at the moment of death. At that moment, it is expected that some supernatural event should occur. At least that's what most followers of this faith expect. So one could argue it isn't just a metaphor or a meditative practice. But then again, we find these gaps in almost all religions. Whatever you make of that is entirely based on your understanding and whether or not this type of Buddhism resonates with you.

Jodo Buddhism

This is the oldest school of Pure Land Buddhism in Japan and was founded by Honen, a Tendai monk who taught that anyone can be reborn in Amida's (Amitabha) Pure Land by simply reciting the nembutsu. Honen insisted that Pure Land should be approached as a separate sect of Japanese Buddhism. His followers included Shinran who founded the Jodo Shinshu School and Ippen who founded the Ji School.

Jodo Shinshu Buddhism

Jodo Shinshu that translates into "True Pure Land School" is a branch of Pure Land Buddhism founded in Japan by the monk Shinran (1173-1262) and organized by Rennyo (1414-99). It is also known as Shin or Shin-shu Buddhism. This school of Buddhism is a lay movement with no monasteries or monks. It is based on absolute devotion to Amitabha (Amida as they call him in Japanese). In Jodo Shinshu, the nembutsu is an act of gratitude, not one of supplication.

According to Religion Facts, Shinran's thought was influenced by an understanding of mappō (the decline of the Dharma) and perceived the era he was living in as being in a degenerate age where beings cannot hope to be able to extricate themselves from the cycle of birth and death through their own power (jiriki). Shinran felt all conscious efforts toward achieving enlightenment and realizing Bodhisattva ideal were rooted in selfish ignorance, and he thought it is better to focus on tariki or reliance on Other Power instead of jiriki. Shin Buddhism has no specific acts to be performed and can, therefore, be considered a practiceless practice. To learn more about this type of Buddhism, please the shared resources under "Pure Land Buddhism."

Chapter 08: The Key Concepts of Buddhism

The goal of Buddhists today remains pretty much the same as it was for the Buddha - to escape and be released from the cycle of rebirth. To escape samsara, end suffering, and attain Enlightenment. In the present day, when a Buddhist reaches that transcendent level of enlightenment (most often done through intense and dedicated meditation) he or she is said to achieve nirvana. Now that you have gained some basic understanding of the history, origin, and different schools of Buddhism, you are undoubtedly ready to dive deep into the core teachings to begin your personal journey. It's vital to keep reminding yourself of the key elements of Buddhism which are: To help you lead a moral life, to help you become mindful and aware of your thoughts and actions and to develop deep wisdom and understanding. Practicing Buddhism included gaining a deep understanding of the human mind and natural therapies (depending on your chosen school) which prominent psychologists across the globe are now discovering to be very advanced and effective.

At the core of the Buddha's teachings or what's commonly known as dharma are The Four Noble Truths. This is what we want to focus more on understanding, but first, let's make sure you understand some of the terminologies that are frequently used in Buddhism.

Karma

Karma is the law of cause and effect that is embedded in dependent origination. It is a universal law that cannot be altered or muted. Buddhism places a great emphasis on Karma. It can be summed up as our actions and the results of those actions. Whether your action is conscious or unconscious, it leaves an imprint on the mind, a sort of "forward momentum" that influences all successive life events.

The choices you make with your mind, body, and speech affects everyone around you, including yourself. Sometimes the results are immediate and obvious, but most of the time, they are not. For example, a butterfly flapping its wings in the Pacific can cause a hurricane in the Atlantic. Ever heard of the butterfly effect? Equally, our actions have consequences far beyond ordinary thinking and carry with them consequences that impact others and us. Gaining awareness of this law helps reinforce our practice of Buddhism, and the reason we have teachings and guidelines is to receive the support we need to create the right conditions for enlightenment. As you continue on your journey, the Buddha's dharma will help modify and instruct your actions (karma) and promote happiness and right conditions for you and others.

Nirvana

Nirvana in Sanskrit or Nibbana in Pali is used to refer to the extinction of desire, hatred, and ignorance and ultimately of suffering and rebirth. It can be translated as "becoming extinguished or blowing out." According to Britannica, the term nirvana has entered the Western culture and is used to refer to a heavenly or blissful state. But from the teachings of the Buddha, we find a different meaning. The Buddha taught that human existence consists of various forms of suffering which keep recurring as we said until one breaks out of the state called samsara. He determined that the cause for this suffering were negative actions and the negative emotions that motivate them, which must be destroyed. If these causes could be eradicated, it follows that there would cease to be any corresponding effect. Therefore, all suffering would cease. This cessation was nirvana. Therefore nirvana was not regarded as a place but as a state of absence, especially the absence of suffering. The details of what exactly is to be expected in this state have been the subject of much discussion over the history of the tradition. What we know is that many people describe it as pure bliss that is unchanging, secure, and unconditioned.

Suffering

The Pali word Dukkha is usually translated to mean suffering, and though many Buddhists feel it isn't an accurate translation, you will see it appearing in many texts and conversation. The Buddha is often quoted as saying, "All I teach is suffering and the end of suffering." Suffering in his teaching doesn't literally mean physical pain, agony or anguish as we generally say in the West. Instead, it is the mental suffering we undergo in our confusion and ignorance of what life is. It presents itself in an array of emotions from happiness and excitement to despair.

According to Buddhism, we are trapped in the cycle of existence known as Samsara (you've read this several times in previous chapters) and so we wander aimlessly, confused, and unaware. This creates an unbearable experience of suffering day and night, year after year, lifetime after lifetime. All because of our tendency to hold on to that which is impermanent and empty. As our desire for pleasure increases, and we are met with the fleeting nature of life that seems to take away the very pleasure that we seek, our experiences grow more unsatisfying and ungovernable.

Buddhist scholar Glenn Wallis had this to say when asked: "what is Dukkha?"

In getting a better feel for the meaning of dukkha, let's place "suffering at one extreme of the spectrum. At the other extreme, let's place qualities such as annoyance, tension, and nondependability. Dukkha, then, can be understood on one end of the spectrum as a subtle, perhaps barely discernible quality of being, and on the other, as a severe mental or physical anguish. A further nuance is added to the term dukkha when we bear in mind that, in the Buddha's view, even a "happy" moment is tinged by dukkha. That is because neither the moment nor the experience is stable. Given this view, what should we call dukkha in our language? Our English term would have to have the following colorings on an increasing scale of intensity.

Faint unsettledness, irritation, impatience, annoyance, frustration, disappointment, dissatisfaction, aggravation, tension, stress, anxiety, vexation, pain, desperation, sorrow, sadness, suffering, misery, agony, anguish. Of course, you may add to this list; there is virtually no end to it. It is obvious that each of these qualities involves some degree of unease, so "unease" is how I translate the term for general usage. (Excerpt from Lion's Roar, What is Suffering? September 8, 2017)

Reincarnation

Famous Buddhist teacher Thich Nhat Hanh offers wise words that help shine light on this often-confusing term. He said, "Reincarnation means there is a soul that goes out of your body and enters another body. That is a prevalent, very wrong notion of continuation in Buddhism. If you think that there is a soul, a self, that inhabits a body and that goes out when the body disintegrates and takes another form, that is not Buddhism. When you look into a person, you see five skandhas, or elements: form, feelings, perceptions, mental formations, and consciousness. There is no soul, no self, outside of these five, so when the five elements go to dissolution, the karma, the actions, that you have performed in your lifetime is your continuation. What you have done and thought is still there as energy. You don't need a soul or a self, in order to continue. It's like a cloud. Even when the cloud is not there, it continues always as snow or rain. The cloud does not need to have a soul in order to continue. There's no beginning and no end. You don't need to wait until the total dissolution of this body to continue - you continue in every moment."

In the Encyclopaedia Britannica, Reincarnation is defined as the rebirth of the aspect of an individual that persists after bodily death. It is also called transmigration or metempsychosis. "Although Buddhism denies the existence of an unchanging, substantial soul or self - as against the notion of the atman it teaches the concept of anatman (non-self) - it holds to a belief in the transmigration of the karma that is accumulated by an individual in life. The individual is a composition of five ever-changing psycho-physical elements and states, or skandhas, i.e., form, sensations, perceptions, impulses, and consciousness and terminates with death. The karma of the deceased, however, persists and becomes a vijnana (germ of consciousness) in the womb of a mother. The vijnana is the aspect of consciousness that is reborn in a new individual." (The Editors of Encyclopaedia Britannica - Reincarnation. January 27, 2017)

Different religions and ancient civilizations have used this term in their own specific way, so it varies in meaning depending on where you learn it. Here in Buddhism, we believe in reincarnation because we uphold the doctrine of karma. Since in karma we know that all actions have consequences, what you do in this present life will have its effects in the next life.

In Buddhism, everything we do becomes Karma. That karma becomes potent, and by natural law, it must come back to us. This is why, in Buddhism, the focus isn't placed on a higher being. It's not a question of proving or disproving God because we believe that's beside the point. Our focus is on making ourselves better individuals. When you accept karma and reincarnation, you take personal responsibility, and it also changes your perspective on tolerance and acceptance of everyone.

How does reincarnation work?

This is a question many new students of Buddhism have. So I think it's only right that we walk through a simple exercise that can help you internalize what reincarnation is.

I want you to relax now, close this book for a bit, and then close your eyes. Mute out the noise coming into your ears. Make sure nothing is touching you, and you're not touching anything. Just sit in the silence for a moment then come back to reading this book so we can move on to the next exercise. Did you actually do it for a few minutes? Okay. Great.

Now, in that state of going "within," can your mind still see, sense, hear, taste, and touch? The answer is yes. You can be able to see a sunset or the beach or smell a rose flower even though they are nowhere in sight.

Next... when you're dreaming and your gross consciousness is completely gone; you're deeply asleep. Can your mind feel, see, hear, smell, taste, and touch? The answer is yes. Dream states (where you're touching, feeling sensing and experiencing things) can feel just as real and profound as your awake state. That's how you can come out of a dream sweating, heartbeat racing and feeling genuinely afraid. Or you can awaken so happy, thrilled, and crying tears of joy about something that happened. Ever experienced that?

That mind that is experiencing all of that whether you are going through your day or deep in sleep is your actual mind. That mind is a temporary resident in this body that you inhabit now. Again, can you remember everything that you did last Monday? You probably can't remember all the details of that day but if you relaxed, sat in the silence with your mind you'd be able to retrieve that memory.

Can you remember everything you did ten years ago? What about the first year of your life? Can you recall the first few weeks after your birth? For most of us, we can barely remember much about the last ten years, let alone the first ten months after birth. But here's the thing. If you took the time and relaxed and talked to a few key people, lots of those memories would pop right back into your consciousness. You may not have the memory of each experience since childbirth at hand, but that doesn't mean they didn't happen or that you didn't do it. The fact that you had cognition at infancy and can recall some of what happened means the same mind you had at infancy is the same mind you had ten years ago and the same mind you have today. That mind never changed. You are the same individual, but your body has changed, perceptions have become sharper, your ability to communicate, etc. has gotten better, but the mind behind all of it is very much one mind. Makes sense?

So if you've had the same mind since birth, what about before birth? What about the 9 months you were in your mother's womb? Science now confirms that unborn babies hear and are affected by everything their mother experiences. Which means, the mind you were born with and grew up with till today, has been active since before birth. And this is where it gets a bit wild - what about before conception?

Do you think you had a mind at the time of conception? Even if this feels too absurd for you, logic will lead us to agree that you must have had a mind at the time of your conception in order to have it during gestation, during birth, and beyond. And this same mind is the one you'll have next Monday, ten months from now, ten years from now until death. So if you're following my train of thought and we've gone as far back as your conception, and you agree you must have had a mind then, doesn't it make sense that your mind existed even before conception? Think about it for a moment. Where was your mind before the conception of this human form?

That is what Buddhism calls, your previous life. Life has to continue. Your mind is on a continuous journey, and everything you liked, disliked, did or didn't do in your previous lives is contained in that one mind. They follow you as you transition from inhabiting one body to the next. The actions you did in mind, body, and speech followed you into this life and are converted into Karma. This is what we learn in Buddhism.

Another excellent example in our society that can help us understand how the mind works is money. Money can be coins, paper, checks, or electronic plastic cards. Money can be converted into various forms, and the mind is very similar. It will take various forms to express itself. Buddhism teaches that by doing breath meditation, we can start recalling experiences from previous lives because even that is just a memory that can be retrieved.

There are many stories of Tibetan lamas who remember their previous lives perfectly. These individuals can remember details like their names, where they used to live etc. and it correlates, and people can find them. Leading Buddhist teacher Zoketsu Norman Fischer summed up the understanding of reincarnation nicely when he said, "For me the most important thing about the teaching of rebirth, the part that seems true and that matters a great deal is that life continues. That is, there is more to our lives than the short lifespan of time between birth and death. The teaching of rebirth tells us that our life and death are significant beyond their appearances, more significant than we know. Being born is important. Dying is important. Death is definitely a hugely important transition, at least as huge as birth. Every moment of life is an important transition. For me, this is what the teaching of rebirth comes down to."

Chapter09: The Four Noble Truths

The Four Noble Truths are considered the foundation of Buddhism. After gaining Enlightenment, the Buddha's first sermon centered on these Four truths, which today form the doctrine of his teachings. Most commonly thought of as - life is suffering; suffering is caused by greed. It ends when we stop being greedy and the way to do that is to follow something known as the Eightfold Path. But I want us to approach and view these truths with more depth. Dukkha is the truth of suffering. Samudaya is the truth of the cause of suffering. Nirodha is the truth of the end of suffering. Magga is the truth of the path that frees us from suffering. Suffering not in the context we are used to here in the West, but in the true sense that was revealed to us earlier. The same way the Buddha meant it.

The First Noble Truth: Dukkha

This explains the nature of Dukkha and is said to have the following aspects. The obvious physical and mental suffering associated with birth, growing old, illness, and dying. The anxiety or stress of holding on to ever-changing things. A sense of dissatisfaction due to the fact that all forms of life are impermanent and without any inner core or substance. Dukkha is anything temporary or conditional. Even something enjoyable is considered as dukkha because it will end. The importance is given to dukkha in Buddhist philosophy often causes new followers to reconsider because it appears to be centered on pessimism. However, it was never intended to present a pessimistic view of life but instead to present a realistic assessment of the human condition. The Buddha was never claiming that all of life is relentlessly awful and negative. In many other sermons, we are told he spoke of various types of happiness. What he wanted us to become aware of is that dukkha touched every area of our lives, including happy times. The Buddha also taught that skandhas are dukkha because even they are impermanent. In other words, the body you identify as yourself is dukkha because it is impermanent and must eventually perish. That doesn't have to be a negative thing. It all depends on your understanding and interpretation of life.

The Second Noble Truth: Samudaya

This explains the origin of dukkha. In the context of the Four Noble Truths, the source of dukkha is identified as craving or thirst (the Pali word is tanha) conditioned by ignorance (the Pali word is avijja). This craving is further explained as: "Craving for sense-pleasures" or kama-tanha. It means craving for objects or sensory pleasures. There is also "craving to be" or bhava-tanha. It means craving to be something, to unite with a particular experience or to dominate over others. Lastly, there is "craving not to be" or vibhava-tanha. It's about craving not to experience the world and to be nothing. In other words, a wish for separation from painful feelings. Ignorance is the deeper root cause behind all dukkha. It refers to the misunderstanding of the nature of the self and reality. The root cause of dukkha is said to be these three poisons: Ignorance (Sanskrit term: avidya or moha), which is the misunderstanding of reality. Attachment (Sanskrit term: raga), which is an attachment to pleasurable experiences. Aversion (Sanskrit term: dvesha), which is the fear of getting what we don't want or not getting what, we do want. Now, from these teachings, one might think Buddhism is against having desires, but that's not accurate. We all know that humanity is continually chasing after external things in search of happiness. And despite this chase, satisfaction is never fully attained. This second truth isn't telling you and me to give up desire and everything we love. The issue here is subtler and requires much insight. What lands us into trouble and suffering is the attachment we have to what we desire. When desire turns into an ungoverned craving, the end result is never good. The Buddha taught that thirst grows from ignorance of the self. In other words, the less you know about who you really are, the more consumed you will be with external things, and the more cravings you'll have. You'll be seeking to experience a sense of security and self-identification. And it will be impossible to satiate that craving permanently. Where do you suppose this idea of "me against the world" comes from?

Buddhist practices help bring about a radical change in perspective. Buddhism is the antidote that cures the void, emptiness, and lack of fulfillment you've struggled with. And in time you'll find it easier to fully live in the moment, experiencing life without judgment, bias, manipulation, or any other mental barriers.

The Third Noble Truth: Nirodha

This is the cessation of dukkha. Many Buddhist teachers like to equate the Four Noble Truths as taught by the Buddha with what happens when you visit a doctor. First, the doctor will tell you what's wrong, what caused the problem and then offer a solution to the problem. In that sense, the first noble truth tells us what the problem is. The second tells us the cause of the problem, and this third one presents the solution to the problem. The Pali word nirodha can be translated to cessation, referring to the cessation of dukkha and the cause of dukkha. It is the cessation of all unsatisfactory experiences and their causes. The end of all suffering. It completely annihilates any repeat of those things.

The solution to dukkha is to stop attaching and clinging to that which is impermanent. Easier said than done though, so how do we do it?

Well, I'll tell you one thing for sure, it can't happen in an instant. There is no magic wand, and your will alone isn't going to be enough. The Buddha taught that through diligent practice, we could put an end to all craving. Cessation should be the goal of your spiritual practice.

From a Buddhist point of view, once you develop a genuine understanding of the causes of suffering in your life (the cravings and ignorance), then you can completely eliminate these causes and ultimately gain freedom from all suffering. When this happens, you become an Enlightened being, and it is said that nirvana or nibanna will become the natural state you experience.

The Fourth Noble Truth: Magga

This Fourth Noble Truth took up most of the sermons that the Buddha gave and for a good reason. As we said before if you pay the doctor a visit, he needs to be able to deliver a full solution so that you come out from there with hope, a cure and a prescription with full instructions on how to apply yourself so the treatment can work. The magga is the prescription on how to apply ourselves so we can end dukkha. It is known as the Eightfold path.

One of the things I treasure about Buddhism is the fact that it isn't a religion that is centered on beliefs but instead on practices. Believing in a god or gods or a doctrine isn't the principal idea; living the doctrine and walking the path is.

The path is eight broad areas of practice. It consists of Right View, Right Intention, Right Speech, Right Action, Right Livelihood, Right Effort, Right Mindfulness, and Right Concentration. These are all interconnected and when developed together lead to the cessation of dukkha and ultimately Enlightenment.

Some people get confused here because they assume that the Noble Eightfold Path is about moving from one level to the next at different intervals. This is misleading. These eight are not separate stages. They are eight significant dimensions of your behavior that need to be developed, controlled, and concentrated together. Your mind, body, words, and actions are dependent on one another and therefore, must be taken together as they define a complete path. This path cannot be fully understood all at once and requires exploration and discipline. It's not a one-time thing or something you do for a specific period; this is a way of life. Without the path, the first three Truths are just theory.

If the doctor prescribed treatment for your disease, and you chose to do nothing about it afterward, the entire session would be meaningless. Why? Because you wouldn't be cured. You would know what's wrong with you and where it came from, but you'd still be sick. Similarly, if you don't practice the Eightfold path, you'd know about suffering and its cause in your life, but you wouldn't be free from it. The practice of the Eightfold path, which is often represented by the Dharma Wheel, is what brings dharma into one's life and makes it bloom.

Dependent Origination in Buddhism

The teaching of Dependent Origination is an essential teaching in Buddhism that says everything is interconnected. It is essential to understanding almost everything about Buddhism. His Holiness, the Dalai Lama, said, "Once we appreciate that fundamental disparity between appearances and reality, we gain a certain insight into the way our emotions work, and how we react to events and objects. Underlying the strong emotional responses we have to situations, we see that there is an assumption that some kind of independently existing reality exists out there. In this way, we develop an insight into the various functions of the mind and the different levels of consciousness within us. We also grow to understand that although certain types of mental or emotional states seem so real, and although objects appear to be so vivid, in reality, they are mere illusions. They do not really exist in the way we think they do."

Everything that is, is because other things are. What is happening now is a continuation of what happened before and will become part of what happens next. Sometimes this principle is called Interdependent Origination, Co-Arising, Conditioned Genesis or Causal Nexus, just to name a few terms. In Sanskrit, the term is Pratitya-Samut Pada. It is a core teaching across all Buddhist sects and schools. We are taught that nothing is absolute. All beings and phenomena exist interdependently. This is especially true for the illusion of self. As beings and phenomena exist, they cause other beings and phenomena to exist. Things and beings perpetually arise and perpetually cease because other things and beings perpetually arise and perpetually cease, and all of this occurs in one vast field or nexus of beingness. It takes a while to wrap your head around this one for sure, so take your time. The first time I learned this, I felt my brain overheating - it was a lot to process all at once.

In Buddhism, there is no teaching of a First or Primary Cause. How all of this arising and ceasing began (whether there was a beginning or not) is never discussed, contemplated, or explained. The Buddha focused and emphasized his teachings on understanding the nature of things as they are rather than speculation of what might have happened in the past or what will come to pass in the future. I hope you're beginning to see that a central theme in Buddhism is present-moment awareness. It's about being fully here and understanding what is here and now.

We taught that things are the way they are because they are conditioned by other things. For example, your childhood, parents, teachers, other people, and phenomena condition you. The same is true for other people and phenomena itself. The Buddha said, "When this is, that is. This arising, that arises. When this is not, that is not. This ceasing, that ceases."

A more common statement we've all heard in the west is, things are the way they are because you are the way you are. Something tells me whoever said it was taking some life lessons from this school of thought.

Dependent Origination is related to the doctrine of Anatman, which dictates that there is no self. Nothing is permanent. We discussed this already in chapter three, so if you're still confused about Anatman, go back and read those first few chapters. What you usually think of, as "yourself" is a temporary construct of the five skandhas - form, perception, mental formations, sensations, and consciousness. So your personality and self-identifying ego is an assembly of phenomena that is the basis for the illusion of a permanent "you" separate and distinct from everything else. The same phenomena were caused to arise and assemble in a certain way because of other phenomena, and they in turn, perpetually cause other phenomena to arise until eventually they will be caused to cease.

In other words, "you" are a phenomenon just as the wave is a phenomenon of the ocean. A wave is the ocean, and although distinct, it cannot be separated from the ocean. When conditions such as strong winds cause a wave, nothing is added to the ocean. When the activity ceases, nothing is taken away from the ocean. In understanding this principle of dependent origination and the impermanence of things, we begin to understand why everything is anicca (impermanent) and anatta (without individual essence). Our ignorance of this truth gives rise to dukkha. See how everything leads to the Four Noble Truths?

The Twelve-linked Chain Of Causation also called Cause and Effect

This is a fundamental teaching of Buddhism. We mentioned earlier in the book, but let's dissect it further now. It is said to be a detailed expression of the Four Noble Truths explaining where the causes of our unhappiness come from. The twelve-linked chain of causation is an explanation of how this three-tiered casual relationship of illusion, karma, and suffering, applies to the reality of our lives.

We learn that unhappiness is rooted in illusion, which is based on earthly desire. Through our thoughts and actions that result from illusion, we create karma, and as a result of that karma, we experience suffering.

In more common language this is referred to as the Law of Cause and Effect. Without a deep comprehension of this, one cannot possibly understand Buddhism or move forward on the path. What we know about the Law of cause and effect is that every effect has a cause and a condition. The cause and condition combine to make an effect. Hence all effects have a cause, all effects have a condition, and there are no exceptions. Translating this back into Buddhist teachings - Good deeds bring good results. Evil deeds bring bad results. Your own deeds will bring about corresponding results without exceptions.

If you want to experience this law of causation in everyday life, think about farming. A farmer plants an orange seed, and when the time is right, he will harvest an orange. If you plant a rose, what would you expect to grow? A rose bush. The farmer can't plant oranges and get watermelons or for you to plant roses and get orchids. Likewise, the pleasant life you desire to produce can only come from a good cause. Our deeds and our actions determine our fates. Never has there been a case where a good deed has produced an adverse effect. Therefore our happiness or unhappiness is rooted in the acts we perform.

In essence, this principle says that no phenomenon, whether outer or inner, cannot occur except as a reaction to a previous cause and that all phenomenon will in turn condition the following results.

The more we can see this, the easier it will be to perceive the interconnectedness of all things. It also helps us to see how we create a world of suffering for others and ourselves as well as how we create happiness. In so doing, we are able to make different choices that enable us to lead lives that reduce suffering for all and ultimately discover freedom.

The twelve links or categories of classic Buddhist doctrine that create the cycle of existence that makes up samsara (the endless circle of dissatisfaction that constitutes the unenlightened life) are:

1. Avidya, which translates to Ignorance.

2. Samskara, which translates to Volitional Action.

3. Vijana, which translates to Conditioned Consciousness.

4. Nama-rupa, which translates to Name and Form.

5. Sadayatana, which translates to The Six Senses.

6. Sparsha, which translates to Sense Impressions.

7. Vedana, which translates to Feelings.

8. Trishana, which translates to Craving or Desire.

9. Upadana, which translates to Attachment.

10. Bhava, which translates to Becoming.

11. Jati, which translates to Birth.

12. Jara-maranam, which translates to Old Age and Death.

We break these links and escape samsara as a result of enlightenment. In the classical Buddhist teachings, these twelve links explain how dependent all things are and the cyclic connection we are all trapped in. It is not a linear path, and if we desire to escape, we just need to break the link at any point because once the link breaks, the chain becomes useless. Again, you'll find different schools of Buddhism interpreting the links in a variety of ways depending on the approach of the teacher. To dive even deeper into each of these twelve links, you can find the recommended learn religions citation on the resource page.

Chapter 10: The Five Precepts Of Buddhism

The five precepts for conduct are the teachings the Buddha would give to everyone, including laypeople. It's the basis of Buddhist ethics but don't make the mistake of thinking of them as commandments (as is often the case in the West). In Christianity, there are the Ten Commandments or the ten things God said everyone must do, and by following these commandments, God would be nice to you. As you know, there's a lot of pushback and negative reactions associated with this idea, so make sure you don't approach these five precepts with any of that thinking. The Buddha taught the five precepts as practices, not commandments. And as practices, the more you follow them, the more you would find yourself being a generally happier person in a generally happier world. The number of precepts if one is a monk runs into the hundreds in some sects but for laypeople, Theravada traditions only these five that are to be seen almost like the baseline for anyone to practice Buddhism. Lay practice amounted to keeping the five precepts because laypeople were not required or even expected to do meditation or any of the more rigorous commitments necessary for the path.

The five precepts are:
- To abstain from taking life.
- To abstain from taking what is not given.
- To abstain from false speech of any kind.
- To abstain from sexual misconduct.
- To abstain from intoxicants (especially alcohol) that tend to cloud the mind.

Buddhists don't have just one set of precepts but the above-mentioned are the most basic. A more literal translation from the original Pali for each would be, " I undertake to observe the precept to abstain from killing, stealing, lying, misusing sex, and abusing intoxicants. Remember the more you train yourself to maintain the five precepts, you're not just following rules, you are teaching yourself to behave as a Buddha would.

Mahayana tradition generally follows a more extended list (Ten Precepts) that is found in the Mahayana Sutra called Brahmajala or Brahma Net Sutra. Here are the Ten Precepts from Mahayana tradition:
- To abstain from killing.
- To abstain from stealing.
- To abstain from lying.
- To abstain from misusing sex.
- To abstain from intoxicants.
- To abstain from talking about others' errors and faults.
- To abstain from elevating myself and blaming others.
- To abstain from being stingy.
- To abstain from being angry.
- To abstain from speaking ill of the Three Treasures.

Some Mahayana Buddhists also vow to uphold what is known as the Three Pure Precepts, which are associated with walking the path of a bodhisattva. They are:
- To do no evil.
- To do good.
- To save all beings.

Developing the Mind and Character with Practice of the Precepts

The first two steps in the process of becoming a lay disciple of the Buddha are: The going for refuge, also known as Sarana gamana, and the undertaking of the five precepts also known as pañca-sila samadana. By taking the first step, you make the commitment to accept the Triple Gem, i.e., the Buddha, the Dharma, and the Sangha (see chapter two and three if you don't recall what they mean), as the guiding ideals of your life. With the second step, you express and demonstrate your determination to bring your actions into harmony with the teachings and ideals of Buddhism through right conduct. To enter the teachings of Buddha, we must pass through the door and "go for refuge," but once we've made that initial commitment, it is necessary to put the teaching into daily practice for the Buddha's teaching isn't a system of salvation by faith. It is not passive but rather active and must be walked daily. The more we practice the five precepts, the more we take responsibility for our lives. Achievement of enlightenment and deliverance is taken away from external forces and gets placed into our own hands. We develop our minds, strengthen ourselves, and move closer to freedom as we realize the goal for ourselves, within ourselves by working upon ourselves with the guidance of the Buddha's instructions.

How the Precepts help you attain Enlightenment

If you really want to understand the critical role the Five Precepts play on your path, you must first study the Four Noble Truths. The Fourth Truth, which offers the Eightfold Path as we discovered, directly connects us to these Five Precepts. The Precepts are connected to the "ethical conduct" part of the Path - Right Speech, Right Action, and Right Livelihood. Without this training and practice, you cannot attain Enlightenment.

Chapter 11: Mindfulness Meditation Practice In Buddhism

Mindfulness is very trendy in Western culture even amongst those who are not interested in Buddhism. Some psychologists have also adopted mindfulness teachings as part of their therapy practices. In Buddhism, mindfulness is one of the most essential practices and is part of the Eightfold path.

What is mindfulness? Some think of it as a state of mind; others view it as a practice. In both cases, it's about cultivating a particular quality and power of the mind. I see mindfulness as being awake and aware of the present moment and continually touching life deeply in all that we do and experience as we go through daily living.

In Buddhism, we are taught that if we want to be truly alive, present and at one with those around us and with the activities we engage in, then we need to practice mindfulness. As you eat, walk, sit, wash dishes, speak to another, work, or whatever else you're doing, you can train yourself to bring mindfulness into each of these activities. The Buddha taught his followers to practice mindfulness all the time, and so must you. In Buddhism, mindfulness goes beyond paying attention to things. It is a pure awareness that is free of judgment and self-reference. In the Satipatthana Suta, we are told that the Buddha taught these 4 foundations of mindfulness of which I will give but a brief and straightforward overview of each, after which I will share tips on how to start practicing them in your daily life.

• Mindfulness of body

This is the first stage where we learn to be mindful and experience the body as - the body. Not a form you're inhabiting, not "my body" just - body. Most introductory mindfulness exercises focus on the breath, teaching us to experience being the breath and the breathing itself without trying to come up with ideas about it. There is also mindfulness of chewing in mindful eating, mindfulness of our steps in walking, etc.

The Buddha suggested we take the time to contemplate deeply on and be mindful of the body in its completeness to become more aware of its selfless, impermanent and conditioned nature so we can begin the process of truly being able to let go. As your ability to maintain awareness increases, you become aware of your whole body, including the elements and internal organs that you often shy away from. In some schools of Buddhism, this exercise might also include an awareness of aging and mortality. Body awareness is incorporated into body practice or movement. This can consist of chanting and rituals depending on the sect, as it is seen as an opportunity to be mindful of the body as it moves and in this simple way we train ourselves to be mindful when we aren't meditating too. In some Buddhist schools, monks and nuns have practiced martial arts as a way of bringing meditative focus into movement. But in your case, the day-to-day activities can be used as "body practice."

• Mindfulness of feelings

The second foundation of establishing a mindfulness practice as taught in Buddhism is to become aware of feelings both bodily sensations and emotions. This stage is extremely important as it deals directly with the three poisons of greed, hatred, and delusion. Why are we taught this? Because in Buddhism, pleasurable feelings lead to attachments such as greed and lust. Painful feelings lead to aversions such as hatred and fear, and neutral feelings lead to delusion, which is also not the true nature of reality. In our day-to-day lives, we usually acknowledge things as either pleasurable or painful. Rarely are we neutral about something. And to do this is to deepen our confusion and perpetuate the chain of suffering.

Through meditation, one learns just to observe emotions and sensations as they come and go. And this is done without any judgment, attachment or self-identification. To state it simply, as I sit there in meditation and become aware of the sensations and feelings I acknowledge, "this is not my feeling and feelings do not define who I am. This is just a feeling."

Of course, this isn't always easy to do, especially when we are worried, stressed, anxious, or in pain. But ignoring those uncomfortable feelings or trying to suppress them is very unhealthy. Having said all of this, I want you to know that Buddhism is not against experiencing joy. What we are taught is to be skillful about such experiences so as not to attach to any pleasurable feeling otherwise that pleasure will soon transform into suffering. For example, I can recall the first time I fell in love. It was pure ecstasy, and everything in my world took on a different tone and color. I felt like I was walking on a springboard because of how elevated my steps were, and nothing could annoy me. Not even rush-hour traffic. What started off as pure joy without attachment quickly turned me into a junkie. I started craving and needing that feeling. A few months later, I fell into a depression, and it took months before I felt a sense of normalcy again. The suffering I experienced was so unbearable it took a long time before I even entertained the thought of dating again.

This is an easy to understand example experience that many of us can relate to. And it can happen with an intimate relationship, a job promotion, the birth of a new child, etc. In fact, if you ask a lot of people who spend months planning a vacation how they felt after it was over, many will say that it created some very uncomfortable feelings. This is the suffering we subject ourselves to when we don't practice mindfulness. We identify with the pleasurable feeling so much and become attached to something transient by natural law. So how do we actually deal with everyday situations like the examples I just shared? By practicing mindfulness. It is possible for you to live in such a way that you experience great peace and joy without attaching or averting things. Of course, this is easier said than done, but that is why we choose to walk the Buddhist path.

• Mindfulness of mind

This is the third foundation of mindfulness as taught by the Buddha. The "mind" or "Citta" in this context doesn't refer to the thinking mind. Citta, as it is called, initially refers to consciousness or awareness. So we can call this mindfulness of consciousness. Sometimes you'll hear the term "heart-mind" when Citta is being translated because it has an emotive quality. This is your awareness that isn't made up of ideas, but that doesn't mean it is pure consciousness. Another way you could look at this is that it refers to your mental states. Thich Nhat Hanh dives deeper into this topic of mental states because they have their own categories and are pretty vast. I don't know if you're aware, but each of the chapters on this book could be books in and of themselves if I was to go deeper into each detail and this particular foundation is no different, so I encourage you to do a little more research if you want to comprehend mindfulness of the mind fully. But a simple way to start practicing this type of mindfulness is to become more aware of the different mental states you experience as you go through the day. Sometimes you might be sleepy, other times restless, stressed, annoyed, angry, fearful, and so on. Learn to observe all these different states as they come and go without judgment or self-condemnation. As you do, it'll be easier to acknowledge where you are and course correct.

• Mindfulness of dharma

This fourth foundation of mindfulness enables us to open ourselves up to the world or at the very least, the world we experience. As we said before, Dharma in Sanskrit can be defined in various ways, but a baseline to use is "natural law" or "the way things are." In mindfulness of dharma, we practice awareness of the inter-existence of all things. It is sometimes called mindfulness of mental objects because all of the myriad things around us exist for us as mental objects. Our recognition and interpretation of things make them as they are. So we practice mindfulness of dharma to make ourselves aware that all things are temporary, without self-essence and conditioned by everything else. This leads us into the doctrine of Dependent Origination that we talked about earlier in the book.

Thich Nhat Hanh said, "living mindfully and with concentration, we see a deeper reality and are able to witness impermanence without fear, anger or despair." How do we do this?

Using mindfulness to get rid of stress and anxiety

Often when we have anxiety about something or when we worry about something, most likely what we're worried about isn't happening in the present moment. When we practice mindfulness, we are bringing ourselves back to ourselves and ultimately back to reality. Try these simple exercises to help you get rid of stress and anxiety.

• A physical mindfulness practice: Walking meditation
This is where you're simply focused on the act of walking. Focus on the way the muscles feel in your body as you move. Keep your attention on your balance and every step that you take.

- A Mental mindfulness practice: Meditation for mindfulness.

Sit comfortably and bring your attention to all of your sensations in the body. Sit in that awareness for a while and then bring your awareness to your surrounding. If there is silence in your environment, sit with that for a little while or if there's a pleasant sound that grabs your attention, sit with that. Finally, bring your awareness and attention back to yourself and focus on your breathing.

- An Emotional mindfulness practice. Volunteer your time, energy, skills, and talents.

Volunteering makes us feel great and gets us out of our own heads. Oftentimes it helps us put aside our issues, anxiety, and worries and gives us a better perspective about where we really are in life.

Benefits of practicing mindfulness

As someone who strives to be the best I can be and to be present in each moment, I'm always keen to learn about scientifically proven new health benefits of practicing mindfulness.

Although Buddhism clearly taught the various benefits one would experience through establishing mindfulness, I think (especially for those of us in the West) it's great to see what science can now prove as well. Below is a combination of both scientifically proven benefits as well as what Buddhists teach.

• Practicing mindfulness leads to a healthier mind. This includes reducing your stress levels, anxiety, depression, and it also enables you to handle conditions in a more productive way. In fact, researchers have found that even one session of mindfulness meditation can result in reduced anxiety.

• Practicing mindfulness also leads to a healthier body. It strengthens your immune system, helps you cope with chronic physical pain and increases your psychological response to stress and negative emotions, making it easier for you to remain grounded.

• Practicing mindfulness increases your awareness and keeps you on the path of awakening. It gives you more clarity and helps ground you more in reality. You become more capable of paying more considerable attention to your mental processes, the physical body, and all the things around you.

• Mindfulness will help you improve all your relationships and social life. Your relationships with strangers, friends, family, and yourself will be enhanced by the greater empathy and compassion that mindfulness allows you to cultivate.

• Mindfulness offers a path to insight. It enables you to cultivate key insights into the nature of phenomena, including oneself, which can lead to greater peace, freedom, and enlightenment.

Mindfulness in your everyday life

Mindfulness can be practiced and cultivated in many different ways. Although mindfulness isn't exclusive to meditation, we find that as far back as the days of the Buddha, mindfulness meditation was the most common technique. Here's a simple four-step exercise to help you practice mindfulness meditation.

Step 1: Become aware of the breath. You can do this anywhere at any time. Simply turn your attention to your breath. Focus on the sensation the breath either at the nostril or the expansion and contraction of the belly as you breathe.

Step 2: Count each in-breath and out-breath. Inhale...one. Exhale...two. Inhale...three. Exhale...four. Count to ten in this way.

Step 3: Acknowledge thoughts, feelings, and sensations non-judgmentally. Know that as you meditate, thoughts, feelings, sensations, distractions will arise and make you lose your concentration on the breath. There's nothing wrong with this, simply observe and do your best to lightly and loosely concentrate on your focal point. Even if you get interrupted every few seconds, you're not doing anything wrong. Simply acknowledge each "interruption" without criticism and judgment.

Step 4: Return to the Breath. Once you've acknowledged the thought, feeling or sensation, simply repeat the process by returning to the breath and beginning your count again from one. Do this until your allocated time is up. Keep doing it until eventually, you will have fewer interruptions when you sit to practice mindfulness meditation.

Aside from mindfulness meditation, you can also bring mindfulness into your everyday life by doing things mindfully. For example, mindful driving, mindful cleaning, mindful eating, mindful body scan, mindful walking, and you can also become more cognizant of intense emotions as they enter your experience.

Starting regular mindfulness of the Buddha practice

Although mindfulness is spreading in the West, it is crucial you know the difference between secular programs that don't even include Buddhism and the mindfulness that was taught by the Buddha. The Buddha taught that mental suffering arises from ignorance (the mind's misunderstanding of the nature of reality, both mental and physical). One of the main tools the Buddha taught for developing insight is the ability to be fully aware in the present moment. He also emphasizes the importance of being able to direct attention and also to retain attentiveness, achieving deep concentration states and cultivating the four divine abidings of compassion, joy, lovingkindness, and equanimity. Besides these tools, he also taught non-meditative practices, which he felt were essential. Practices such as sila (ethical behavior), dana (generosity) and nekkhamma (renunciation), each of which plays a crucial role in developing insight and allowing you to stay on the noble eightfold path.

The Buddha's teaching on mindfulness serves one purpose, and that is, to end suffering. Mindfulness practice, also known as sati enables us to go beneath the surface level of our moment-to-moment life experiences, which are clouded with emotions and habitual thinking. This allows us to see the truth of what is happening. The distinct difference between Buddha's mindfulness and secular mindfulness is that he doesn't teach it as a standalone skill. Instead, it is part of the eightfold path that leads to the realization of the Four Noble Truths and the end of suffering.

In your daily life, your Buddha's mindfulness will help you see clearly what needs to be done, what you are capable of doing, and how that relates to the larger truths. You are to apply mindfulness to your work and personal affairs through wise speech, wise action, and wise livelihood. This is why you often see the Pali phrase - samma sati - being used when speaking of the Buddha's mindfulness. It translates to "wise mindfulness." Mindfulness in your daily practice should support the moment-to-moment intention not to cause harm, to be kind and to renounce those thoughts and actions that lead to heedlessness. Divorced from this wise intention and wise understanding, mindfulness is aimless and therefore not the Buddha's. The mindfulness taught by the Buddha, which you must practice every day is of a particular kind. One that is wise, non-harming, and forward leading.

To act with mindfulness in every moment requires regular practice. A simple exercise you can start this practice today is called the three-minute breathing exercise.

First. Simply notice what's going on right now in your mind. Notice the thoughts, images, or emotions.

Second. Bring your attention to your breathing. Notice the rise and fall of the chest or the belly as you breathe.

Third. Expand your awareness out into the body. Begin to notice any physical sensations. Notice also the contact between body and chair or cushion and mat. Notice the contact between clothes and body.

Commit to doing this for three minutes, three times a day. It is advised to establish specific times throughout the do for this practice. In this way, whether you are at home, at work, at school, or anywhere else, you can continuously train the mind to be mindful.

Chapter 12: Making Mindfulness Part Of Your Life

Vietnamese Buddhist monk Thich Nhat Hanh teaches mindful living as the path to self-understanding and inner peace. He encourages all Buddhist practitioners to see that every moment in life allows us to gain insight into the self. You can make mindfulness part of your life by training your mind to practice it as much as possible. The more you cultivate this skill, the more it will serve you in countless ways for the rest of your life.

Bhikkhu Bodhi teachers that mindfulness is one of the critical ingredients in meditation practice. Since mindfulness is practiced within the context of the Buddhist system of meditation, it goes hand in hand with clear comprehension, and that involves an assessment and evaluation of one's mental states.

Creating your meditation and yoga space

Certain conditions are helpful for the practice of mindfulness, meditation, and yoga. When we create the right environment, it becomes easier to commit and enjoy the experience. Even if your practice space is only a small section of your apartment, make sure it has a feeling of upliftedness and sacredness. Declutter and remove anything that doesn't serve either purpose or design in your sacred space. Choose colors that are calming and don't forget to accessorize your space appropriately. You can use scented candles, incense, aromatherapy spray, and some cool lighting to add a welcoming, sacred softness to the area.

Try to choose a spot that is not too noisy and where you won't get easily disturbed, distracted, or provoked into negative emotions. Whenever you get irritated, frustrated, worried, or experience feelings like jealousy and anger, your practice will be affected so bear that in mind if you choose to attend classes outside your home.

Chapter 13: Benefits Of Buddhism Practices

In Buddhism, the ideal we all strive to attain is to selflessly act to alleviate suffering wherever it appears. That doesn't mean it's easy to do and I know some will argue it is impossible, but regardless the goal remains the same. In a world filled with pain, suffering, chaos, loneliness, disease, lack, and conflict, following the path of the Buddha has never felt so appealing. If like me you arrived at a point in life where you needed a radical transformation, then I hope you will find that Buddhism has something to offer you.

As Buddhist practitioners, we are taught that Buddhism is about living the path; it's about working on ourselves, our minds, and seeking to know the truth for ourselves. Buddhism is more than just a religion or a spiritual practice. It is also self-mastery and a lifestyle that encompasses the mind and body. Another way of looking at this would be to see yourself as a scientist. Buddhism invites you to become your own specialized scientists running experiments in your mind and applying practices that help you find your truth. Through mental training, concentration, and present moment awareness, you are destined to reach enlightenment. With this knowing, can we, therefore, assume that practicing Buddhism will have many benefits in our mental, emotional, and physical health?

I believe so. Modern science seems to agree with this idea as well, and many researchers are taking a keen interest in studying Buddhist practitioners with the aim of understanding how "living the path" can help enhance human living. Here is just a handful of benefits mental, physical, spiritual, social, and overall well-being you can expect to enjoy as you choose to walk the path.

- Mindfulness meditation is an integral part of Buddhism. As a result, one who meditates daily tends to maintain calmness, eliminate stress and anxiety. Many studies, as well as my own experience, prove that mindful meditation can reduce and ultimately eliminate mood disorders, depression, high blood pressure, and a host of other diseases. In other words, a mind is calm scares away any dis-ease. Some studies show Buddhists who are experienced in meditation are least fearful. They aren't frazzled by anything and rarely experience shock, anger, frustration, etc. The next time you're stuck in traffic - bring to mind the image of a Buddhist monk and try to imagine how he would respond to that same situation. It's a great way to shift your energy into a calm state.

- Taking personal responsibility helps you step into your power. When you know you are completely in charge of your life, you can't approach anything the same way. There's a certain confidence that enters your consciousness as you learn to take full responsibility for your life. You stop blaming people, pointing fingers, or waiting for a savior to come and change your conditions. That feeling of being in charge is priceless, and it will make you less dependent on motivation and more "generated from within," which is what we all need more of.

The Buddha said, "The mind is everything, what you think, you become." When you start thinking, "I can do this," guess what happens?

• As a Buddhist practitioner, you will have to stay away from any and all intoxicants. This is one of the five precepts all followers must observe. Therefore alcohol, drugs, tobacco, and other addictive substances will never cloud your mind or mess with your health. To me, this is hugely beneficial, especially in today's world where addiction has become such a huge struggle. Intoxicants of any kind are harmful to your health. Hence by following the five precepts, you are not only staying on the right path to enlightenment, but you're also protecting your body and mind.

• Practicing Buddhism helps you understand and demonstrate equanimity. This empowers you to connect with other people and to treat every person with respect. Superiority and inferiority do not exist; though you'd have a hard time believing that if you look around how society is set up. But we know the deeper truth. Humanity is all one. The only responsibility you have as a human being is to render help to others. This is a fundamental teaching in Buddhism that creates a fantastic ripple effect when practiced daily. Let me give you a quick example that we can all relate to.

A friend told me of this story a few weeks ago. He walked into Starbucks to get a Frappuccino and the lady taking his order did the strangest thing. She asked for his name as usual, then punched out the cash register, issued a receipt and handed it to him. Puzzled, he looked at it and said, "I haven't paid for it yet." She responded, "Yes, I know. But the woman before you asked to pay for the person behind her in line. And she also didn't pay for her coffee because the person in front of her had done the same thing. You see, this morning a man came in here with $20, bought himself a coffee and said, he wanted to pay for the next person who comes in line. So I thought I'll just carry it forward until the change is over, but that was three hours ago, and people keep buying each other coffee. How crazy is that?"

I got so thrilled when I heard this story; I've shared it with everyone since. This demonstration of generosity might be small scale because it was one local coffee shop in a small town, but size doesn't matter. We can learn so much from acts like these. It demonstrates how one person, doing the right thing, can impact so many. I don't know if that generous Starbucks customer is a Buddhist, but by his practice, he is showing the way by which we can start building cities, nations, and a world that is generous, thoughtful and open. This is the fundamental teaching of Buddhism as well.

- Practicing Buddhism awakens you to the Dharma, which also impacts how you co-exist with people and the natural environment. Following the story I just shared, can you also see how dharma comes into play? The Dharma points out that the environment we live in matters a lot. We also learn that every cause has an effect and that if we want to create good results, we must first plant good seeds. As we lead a healthy, kind, generous lifestyle being mindful of others and our environment, we cease to bring harm to our planet and each other. In so doing, we create harmony in the environment. We cannot live in harmony with nature and its components unless we practice the dharma and change.

Conclusion

The journey of Buddhism and the path to enlightenment is long and very intimate. Only you know when you are ready to walk the path. It is a path of awakening and practicing present-moment self-awareness. In modern society, we have become trapped in self-identification that is limited to our family names, our intellectual expressions, or how much money is in the bank. For example, you might say, "I am a student studying psychology, I have two sisters and live in California." This isn't false, but it's not all that you are. Few of us take the time to contemplate the real nature of our existence. Even fewer are brave enough to ask the question, "Who am I?" This is what Buddhism encourages us to pursue. The understanding of who we are and the true nature of things. It's about self-awareness. Learning to understand why you feel what you feel, why you behave as you do and perceive as you do is the first step to heightened self-awareness. Once you begin to understand this concept, you have the opportunity and freedom to change things about yourself, enabling you to create the life that you genuinely want. Having absolute clarity about the true nature of life and your relationship with life is very empowering. It gives you the confidence needed to navigate this human journey.

The education that will be needed for you to go from beginner to someone who has a fair understanding of the Buddha's teaching will continue to unfold as you begin walking the path. Even with all I have shared in this book, I barely scratched the surface of all there is to learn about Buddhism tradition. The deeper you go, the richer it gets and the more complex. This book is condensed and simplified by design. It doesn't need to make sense all at once and should be studied several times over until you feel led to taking the next step, which is, choosing the right school for you.

We have learned about the foundations of Buddhism, the backstory and journey of Prince Siddhartha, turned monk Gautama, who ultimately became the Buddha. The teachings he shared with the world thousands of years ago have evolved, and so has this religion, but the essence of what he taught and believed in remains the same. We are all here, moving through an ever-changing world, and it is our duty to train our minds to remember the truth about who we are and what life is. We must take full ownership of our thoughts, bodies, actions, and behaviors. Underlying all these intense and hard to understand concepts, what stands out to me so strongly is the need to be more loving, kind, and compassionate with oneself and then with others. Choosing to commit to the Buddha's teaching is an act of self-love in my opinion because it's you saying that you are fed up of trapping yourself in falsehood and superficial things. It is, in fact, you choosing to love yourself. As you seek enlightenment, freedom, and understanding of Truth, you are, in fact, choosing to open up to real unconditional love.

The truth about the nature of reality is something we all deserve to know. Whatever your current conditions might be, if you want inner peace, freedom, and enlightenment, Buddhism has something to offer you.

In the words of Buddha, "you can search throughout the entire universe for someone who is more deserving of your love and affection than you are yourself, and that person is not to be found anywhere. You, yourself, as much as anybody in the entire universe deserve your love and affection."

Additional Study Resources

http://www.findingdulcinea.com/guides/Religion-and-Spirituality/Buddhism.pg_00.html

http://www.bbc.co.uk/religion/religions/buddhism/subdivisions/tibetan_1.shtml

Learn religions: https://www.learnreligions.com/what-is-the-buddha-dharma-449710

Going for refuge and the precepts: https://www.accesstoinsight.org/lib/authors/bodhi/wheel282.html#ref

Learn religions: O'Brien, Barbara. "The Twelve Links of Dependent Origination." Learn Religions, Apr. 17, 2019, learnreligions.com/inks-of-dependent-origination-449745.

What type of Buddhism is right for you? Learn more: https://www.learnreligions.com/which-school-of-buddhism-is-right-for-you-449972

Learn more about Mahayana tradition: O'Brien, Barbara. "How Mahayana Buddhism Is the Great Vehicle." Learn Religions, Apr. 27, 2019, learnreligions.com/mahayana-buddhism-overview-450004.

How Buddhism came to Tibet: O'Brien, Barbara. "How Buddhism Came to Tibet." Learn Religions, Apr. 17, 2019, learnreligions.com/how-buddhism-came-to-tibet-450177.

Amitayurdhyana Sutra visualization video: http://purelandbuddhism.info/amitayurdhyana-sutra/

Pure land Buddhism: "Pure Land Buddhism." ReligionFacts.com. 19 Nov. 2016. Web. Accessed 13 Jul. 2019.

<www.religionfacts.com/pure-land-buddhism>

www.ingramcontent.com/pod-product-compliance
Lightning Source LLC
Chambersburg PA
CBHW071238070526
44583CB00017B/2231